Courageous

A Trailblazer's Journey to the
Far Side of the World

DR. DELCIE PALMER

Trilogy Christian Publishers
A Wholly Owned Subsidiary of Trinity Broadcasting Network
2442 Michelle Drive
Tustin, CA 92780

For information, address Trilogy Christian Publishing
Rights Department, 2442 Michelle Drive, Tustin, Ca 92780.
Trilogy Christian Publishing/ TBN and colophon are trademarks of Trinity Broadcasting Network.

For information about special discounts for bulk purchases, please contact Trilogy Christian Publishing.

Manufactured in the United States of America

10 9 8 7 6 5 4 3 2 1

Library of Congress Cataloging-in-Publication Data is available.

ISBN 978-1-64773-015-4 (Print Book)
ISBN 978-1-64773-016-1 (ebook)

Disclaimers

————

Some names have been changed. Some identifying characteristics and details of certain individuals may have been changed. Some timelines were condensed. Details of this book were compiled from a combination of journal entries, and memory. Though, in some instances, it has been several years, a good faith effort was made to be accurate in recollecting details.

This book, and consequently, each chapter, is for educational and entertainment purposes only. It is sold with the understanding that the author and publisher is not engaged in offering any type of legal, psychological, or other professional services.

The author and publisher shall not be liable for any emotional, psychological, physical, or other types of damages, including but not limited to consequential, special, direct, indirect, or incidental damages. You are responsible for your own choices and the consequences of your actions.

Dedication

———

Dedicated to my grandmother Bernice Bogle Creary, the ultimate trailblazer! It is also dedicated to my great-great-grandfather, the Honorable Paul Bogle for setting a high standard of faith. Finally, this book is dedicated to Jesus, for His amazing heart, and in celebration of the incredible gift of salvation to all those who believe.

Introduction

———

When I got my first professional job at a local college several years ago, I was terrified. I was fresh out of college and didn't have any history to suggest that I could do the job. I managed to convince the people during the interview that I was competent, but did I have it in me?

The night before I was to begin work, I dreamt that I was sitting in a cafeteria when a woman rushed in and stopped in front of me. She had a message from God. "I'm glad I found you here," she said. Then she added, "God said, 'Courageous.'"

He wanted me to know that I was on His mind, and that He could see that I was frightened at the prospect of starting a brand new job with a whole new level of responsibility. He cared enough to send an angel while I was sleeping to speak a word of encouragement into my heart.

Courageous! That's the message of this book, and I believe that's God's word to you. Whatever your situation, be courageous! God is with you and will help you as you trust in Him! And I hope that you see from the stories in this book that He is merciful, and he knows exactly how to help you in a storm.

God is faithful.

I am the evidence.

パーマー

A Trailblazer's Journey to:
JAPAN

For the eyes of the Lord run to and fro throughout the whole earth, to show Himself strong on behalf of those whose heart is loyal to Him...

—2 Chronicles 16:9, NKJV

1

Tokyo

I'm nervously watching the kidnapper as he weaves the car through the narrow Japanese streets, and I begin to pray!

Just two hours earlier, I was standing on a train platform in Osaka waiting for an overnight train to Tokyo. It was the first day of my vacation from the high school where I was a missionary and teacher, and I was looking forward to a weekend in the city. What I really needed was rest; I was exhausted. But what I got at the end of the day was one of the most dangerous moments of my life!

As I stood on the train platform, looking toward a black tunnel for signs of the train, I felt uneasy. Maybe it was the prospect of traveling alone, or maybe it was the usual strangeness of being a foreigner in a new country; whatever it was, it left me feeling restless.

To occupy myself, I rehearsed the weekend plans in my mind. I'd arrive in Tokyo around 6 a.m., check into my hotel, have breakfast, then head out for a little relaxation and sightseeing. Somewhere in the day, I would catch up on my sleep. At least that was the plan, but it all started to unravel around midnight when the train rolled into the station. My faith was about to be tested, along with my courage and my trust in God, as I entered the first challenge of the night.

When the train doors opened and I stepped onboard, it looked like a scene from a science fiction movie. The cabin is filled with Japanese men seated and staring straight ahead, with me, the only woman, a Jamaican, standing in the middle of the isle, clutching a large shopping bag and searching for an empty seat. *An overnight train with no empty seats?* I try not to look surprised as I head to the front of the cabin and find a spot to stand near the door. *Six hours.* The thought flickers across my mind.

Within minutes, the train is cutting through sleepy little villages in the suburbs of Osaka. My eyes start to daze over as I stare into the night flanking the landscape. Somehow, the darkness creates a canopy for my thoughts. In the silence, I slowly admit to myself that nothing about this night is working—that it's crazy to try to stand all night on a moving train!

I think about the little money I have to spend for the trip and what it would mean if I got off the train before reaching Tokyo. I'd lose my ticket. I'd have to dip into my savings for a hotel, and I would have to spend more money on another ticket in the morning.

After about an hour, I decide to cut my losses and get off at the next stop to find a hotel and get some well needed rest! With no phone, I have no way of searching for a hotel. My plan is to simply wing it.

And like the doctor comes up to you when it's your turn to get the needle, the next stop comes, and so I stand at the door waiting for it to open, and when it does, I step out, and…Whoa!

Dim overhead lamps!

Dingy walls.

A morbid feeling.

Where is this place?

The station is totally deserted! If I weren't so tired, I would have gotten back on the train, but before I could react, the doors slam shut behind me, the way it does in a bad movie, and the train is rolling out of the station. *That was the last train for the night!*

The train now gone, I glance around at the dark stone walls of the station in search of an exit. Seconds later, I spot a narrow flight of stairs to my left, hurry over to it, and make my way toward the parking lot, hoping that at least there, I might find a taxi, a person or two, or catch sight of a hotel; but as I reach the top stair and look around, I feel a chill.

The parking lot is totally deserted! There are no taxis, no people, just a string of houses covered with shadows from the moonlight; a town in deep sleep except for me standing there, alone in the empty lot in dead silence.

Just then, as it does when it shouldn't, the worst possible thoughts run through my mind. That Ms. Jones during my missionary training for example, and her story of women disappearing from Japan during their missionary work ring in my memory as if she spoke them to me an hour ago, but it was over a year ago.

As I stare into the empty dark town, I push back the fear. After all, other people get abducted, not me! Still, I have a strange stirring in my belly.

I was trying to think of what to do next, trying to stay calm, when suddenly, I felt someone behind me! I turned to see a little Japanese woman wearing a berry colored kimono. Her hair was pulled back in a bun, and she had a high forehead and sunken dark eyes, making her look a bit ghostly.

I didn't stop to analyze—what's an elderly Japanese woman doing in a deserted train station in the middle of the night? I was just relieved to have company. I hurried over to her and tried to piece together a few sentences in Japanese. As I breathed out that first sentence, I had no idea I was stepping into a trap!

"Sumimasen, hotel, oneigai shimasu...?" The old woman looked at me and smiled. I smiled back. After a few seconds, I tried again. "Hotel?"

Without a word, she nodded politely, walked to the far end of the train station and disappeared behind a brick wall, leaving me standing alone again, looking at deserted streets in front of me, and the empty train station behind me. *God, now what?*

A minute or so later, to my relief, the old woman re-appeared with a young woman, maybe around age twenty-five.

"Do you need help?" the young woman asked in fairly good English.

"Yes. You speak English!" *I'm saved!*

"Yes, of course. I can help you. You're looking for a hotel?"

"Yes. Thank you. Is there one around?"

"Yes, of course. I can take you."

"Take me?"

"Well. I know where there is one, but not around here."

"Oh."

"Sorry. But you can still find one. Just not around here."

"Where is the closest one?"

She looked fidgety for a minute, shaking her hands as if she had crabs stuck to her fingertips.

"I don't know how to say it in English. But I can take you." She motioned to a white four-door Toyota parked near the station entrance. A car I noticed for the first time.

"What's your name?" I was stalling. I needed time to think.

"My name is Youkei."

Youkei looked so much like one of my students at the high school where I was a missionary and teacher. She was soft spoken and had a kind face. We chatted for a few minutes about my job at the school and I found out she was a college student in the area.

As I listened to her, my head felt light; the sort of lightheartedness that happens when I'm running on no sleep, no energy, and lots of fatigue. I looked around again for a taxi. Nothing. *I'm too tired for this.*

I took a moment to weigh my options. I could stay alone at the station until trains begin to run again in the morning; I could walk the creepy, dimly lit streets until I found a public place to sit until daybreak, or I could take Youkei up on her offer to take me to the hotel where I could get a good night's sleep.

Youkei was waiting patiently for an answer. Finally, I pushed reason aside. We both weighed around 120 pounds, so I didn't think she'd try anything.

"Okay," I said.

She smiled at me eagerly and then waved to someone who seemed to suddenly appear behind us! He was a stern-looking Japanese man, maybe in his early thirties. He walked right past me and immediately went over to the Toyota, got into the driver's seat and shut the door. I thought maybe it was obvious to him that I was a foreigner and he didn't speak English, so he didn't want to bother greeting me. Still, it made me uneasy. I turned to the young woman.

"I don't want to put anyone out."

"Put anyone out?" She looked confused.

This is crazy. I can't go with these people. I don't even…

"It's okay," Youkei said, interrupting my thoughts. "He knows where it is. It's not very far. We will take you there," she said smiling.

I felt intoxicated with exhaustion.

"I could take a taxi," I said to myself, looking at the empty taxi stand before me, then to the woman, "I hate to inconvenience you." I wanted to believe her. *I'm overreacting. I'm just tired.*

"There are no taxis now. They stop running at midnight. It's okay." She pointed to her right. "The hotel is somewhere over there, maybe fifteen blocks—a long walk, but a short ride by car. Really, it's okay. I am happy to take you there. It's only a five-minute drive."

To this day, I can't fully explain how she managed to talk me into getting into the back seat of the car, but there I was with my shopping bag on the seat beside me.

Youkei smiled as she scooted in the front seat next to the man. She looked over at him for what seemed like a long time, almost as if looking in his face for a reaction. "This is my cousin, Hiroshi," she said nervously. Then she giggled as if hardly believing her own ears.

Her sly giggle hit me like cold water thrown in my face! Alarms started going off in my head! Before I could react, Hiroshi started the car, drove out of the parking lot, and was whipping down deserted streets.

Youkei and Hiroshi stared straight ahead, never saying a word to me or to each other. Then, I had a revelation! It was as if God opened my understanding and I knew what was going on!

My senses were miraculously sharp, and I could identify something looming in the car like a bad vapor, but it wasn't a vapor, it was a spirit, and not just one spirit, but several—the spirit of death, the spirit of pornography and the spirit of violence were flowing out of Youkei and Hiroshi like a sickening odor! I knew by the Spirit of God that Youkei and Hiroshi were predators! All I could think was: "Jesus." He was my only way out!

The sleepiness I felt earlier was now a memory! I sat up straight. As the car sped through the empty streets, I was thinking fast and trying not to panic. Hiroshi had the road all to himself and was whipping along at about 50 mph. *When he stops the car, I'm jumping out!* That was my plan. Then, just bad luck, all the lights were green, and they stayed green. I clutched my bag beside me with my passport and money.

I prayed to Jesus. *Need a red light, Lord. Need a red light, a red light, a red light!* I saw all green lights! Hiroshi kept whipping through them, picking up speed now. Then, I saw my worst nightmare—the on ramp to the highway just after the next green light!

I knew if he got on that ramp I was finished! There would be no houses, no people at 2:00 AM, just open road and me in the back of a car with two lunatics in the front. *This can't happen!*

The car was speeding forward!

I held my breath and watched the last green light before the on ramp. Just a few blocks away, the light stayed green. "*Red light Jesus, red light Jesus, red light…red light!*" It stayed green, green, green, green, then suddenly orange and red! Abrupt stop!

My captors kept quiet the entire time, looking straight ahead and not saying a word to me or each other. I knew I had to stay calm. A Spirit of reason came over me. It was as if Jesus arrived in the car and said, "Fear not. I'm here! Now, listen to Me! You have ten seconds. Get out the car!"

I didn't want Hiroshi to see me getting out the car and speed through that light. Only five seconds left. I grabbed onto the door handle. Four seconds. "Well, hate to inconvenience you," I said, faking calmness. Two seconds. "Thanks anyway but I can walk from here." I swung the door open and was halfway out the car, when—

Youkei quickly said something to Hiroshi, and—

He reached back and tried to grab me! He just missed my arm but grabbed my bag by the handle! *My passport and my money to get home are in the bag!* I yanked the bag, tearing it from his hand, and ran from the car!

I ran up the deserted street, clutching my bag, while looking behind me to see if Hiroshi was chasing me! I could see him checking his rear-view mirror, watching me, weighing his chances of catching me, but neither one of them got out of the car.

Then, I saw a neon sign of a Denny's restaurant a block up on my right. As I hurried up to it, I saw lights on inside, people smiling, drinking, chatting.

I hurried inside the restaurant, still breathless and shaking. I sat down, my heart doing flips in my chest. I realized I was nearly abducted! I tried to calm my breathing.

"Thank you, Jesus," I said under my breath. "You saved my butt."

When the waitress came to take my order, I tried to focus and managed to order a cup of tea.

The restaurant only had a handful of people, but it was well lit, and at least I felt safe.

I sipped my tea and sat there until daylight.

Welcome to the segment of the chapter fondly referred to as the "Faith-Bridge Café." It's an "on the page" café experience for all you trailblazers out there! It's where we can "meet" to reflect on what happened in the preceding story. I suspect some readers might want to grab a cup of coffee or tea as we ponder what happened here.

When I went to Japan as a missionary, I knew I would be facing dangers, but I felt called to serve God in the mission field. I was informed of the risks. I tried to make good decisions, but in a moment of weakness, I slipped up. I was fortunate that God was with me! So, when I got in a car with two strangers in the middle of nowhere, He showed up and pulled me out of trouble!

God at His best—as I was being kidnapped, He schooled me on exactly what to do to escape the danger. I knew I needed to stay calm and keep my attention on Him!

A Spirit of "courage" came over me. What I felt at the time was more than adrenalin. Courage is "the ability to do something that you know is difficult or dangerous."[1] I also felt a sharpened sense of awareness and reasoning, and somehow, God managed to keep me from panicking!

If I had started screaming at my captors saying, "Pull over, let me out. Why are we going on the highway?" what a mess that would have been. Instead, God trumped all the negative forces in the car and helped me to stay focused on the name, Jesus! In other words, it was possible for me to receive deliverance because I shifted my focus away from my captors. My prayer was simply, "Red light, Jesus!"

Also, the Spirit of God provided information. My senses were enhanced in the spirit-realm, so I could understand the nature of what was going on "beneath the surface."

I clearly identified what I would call a spirit of pornography, a spirit of violence, and the spirit of death—the real forces behind Youkei and Hiroshi. It brings light to the phrase, "For we do not wrestle against flesh and blood, but against principalities, against powers, against the rulers of the darkness of this age, against spiritual *hosts* of wickedness in the heavenly *places*" (Ephesians 6:12, NKJV).

At the moment of escape, I knew I should casually get out the car. I knew too, that I shouldn't just get out, but I needed to keep the captors calm, or at least confused, so that talking calmly to them as I opened the door caught them off guard.

Fortunately for me, Hiroshi didn't speak English, and by the time Youkei translated that I was in fact fleeing the vehicle, I was already halfway out the car and had enough momentum to separate myself from the scene.

It may not make sense to some reading this story that I was also determined to take my bag with me in the face of so much danger, but in the middle of nowhere in a foreign country, passport and money take on new relevance. God helped me recover all!

In the end, my life was a prize to me because God was with me. Jesus served as Hero, Warrior, and Guard and effectuated an escape by equipping me in the moment with supernatural courage and understanding!

I learned that His character and strong right arm will never fail me! He has a great heart and He is ready to help those who trust in Him. Thank You, God!

* * * * * * *

Whatever you are facing in life, whatever is challenging you, remember, the secret to every escape from danger or harm is to cling to the name of Jesus: "The angel of the Lord encamps all around those who fear him, and delivers them" (Psalm 34:7).

> For the eyes of the LORD run to and fro throughout the whole earth, to show Himself strong on behalf of *those* whose heart *is* loyal to Him… (2 Chronicles 16:9, NKJV)

God won't ever fail you as you trust in Him!

By the way, if you're traveling anywhere on planet earth, you might want to refuse ride from strangers, no matter how sweet or innocent they seem. Better safe than sorry. I'd also suggest not allowing yourself to get to the point of exhaustion where your reasoning might be compromised. Plan ahead and use wisdom.

And don't beat yourself up if the road is tougher than you imagined. Give yourself credit for trying (I felt God's attention on this). When people step out in ministry they sometimes get a lot of pushback, run into opposition and even danger; then they might doubt their calling. But there is something to be said about the person who takes the step in the first place. Some never try. Be counted among the courageous, among those who lean on God and move forward—and in those tough points in the road, pray. God cares about you!

Safe trailblazing!

2

Japan

Mama (my grandmother) is seated on my family's living room couch in New England, looking at the fire blazing in the fireplace. She glances up at me as I walk over and sit next to her.

"Mama, I'm going to Japan, tomorrow," I said. I was speaking of my first trip to Asia to join a missionary team at an all-girl's high school.

In all the years I've known Mama, she's never spoken much, and this day is no different. She lifts her hand and rest it on my head.

"God go with you," is all she says, and then she smiles at me. It would be the last time I'd see her, and the last words she'd speak over my life. "God go with you," she said.

The night before the trip, I slept very little. I sat alone thinking over my decision. I was going to the far side of the world to share my faith in God. I was new in my commitment to God and well meaning, but as I sat there looking at the fire in the fireplace, I was troubled by the question: "What do I know about Jesus?" That question haunted me. Do I really know anything about Him?

I suddenly felt anxious. Backing out seemed like a really good idea. *Maybe I shouldn't go. I could call the missionary office and back out.* I brushed off those thoughts, and dozed off around 1:00 a.m. *I said I would go and so I will. What's the worst that can happen?*

The next day, on board Japanese Airlines (JAL), as I settled into my seat, I looked at the magazines in the seat pocket to see if they were written in Japanese or English (I found both), then buckled my seatbelt. I watched as other passengers struggled to get their carryon into the overhead bin. I was happy mine fit snugly under the seat in front of me.

After a few minutes, a blonde man around age thirty-five sat beside me, wearing a white shirt and black pants. He smiled. I smiled back. He was rather ordinary, except he seemed stuffy and serious, making me feel a bit uneasy.

"I've been to Japan twice," he reached out a hand to me; I shook it weakly.

"My first time."

"Oh. Vacation?"

"No. Work." I wasn't sure I wanted to become too familiar with someone on the fourteen-hour flight from Boston to Tokyo; but as I looked around at the sea of Japanese faces and saw that I was one of only a handful of non-Japanese on the plane, I suddenly felt a bit of camaraderie with the blonde stranger. "I'm a missionary, and a teacher," I said.

"Oh. A teacher? What will you be teaching…let me guess, math?"

"God forbid. Oral English."

"Oral English? What's that?"

"I teach public speaking, basically, to high school students."

"Going to save the world?" His question caught me off guard.

"What?"

"You said you were a missionary."

His tone made me nervous. I thought back to the stories I heard during my missionary orientation of women getting dragged off to prison, or some disappearing during their missionary work.

"No, I'm not going to save the world." There was some impatience in my voice.

"Thought you said you were a missionary?" He said after grunting—a sort of coy, sly grunt.

"Yeah. I am." I wished I hadn't gotten into the conversation. "But my focus will be mostly on teaching," I said, hoping to end the discussion.

"That's what they want us to think," he said. *Us? What's he talking about?* Suddenly I realized that we were talking about two different things, and that what was in his mind was different from what was in my mind.

I reached into my purse, pulled out my headphones, put them on, and blocked him out for the next fourteen hours.

When I first sat down, I had hoped to get some sleep, but I was awake now. *What have I gotten myself into? I'm going to be on the other side of the planet. I can't go to my family for help. What if they don't like me?*

I thought back to my missionary orientation. One of the orientation leaders was a skinny black woman named Ms. Jones. "You have to realize that they're not all going to like you," she said one day during lunch. I stopped eating my tuna sandwich and looked up at her. "They treat blacks in Japan like they do here." My heart sank! That's not what I wanted to hear.

After four in-flight movies and three meals, JAL was circling over Tokyo. From the night sky, Tokyo looked like any other city to me—specks of light against a mysterious black landscape. Minutes later, JAL landed, and a tired crew prepared us to disembark. As the plane rolled to a stop and the fasten seat belt signs went off, people poured into the isle and started to grab their bags from the overhead compartment.

I was glad when the blonde man ignored me, grabbed his bag from the overhead and headed toward the front of the plane. I let him get a little distance away then I stood to exit my seating area, while clutching my carry-on. At that moment, a Japanese man, around fifty, with a large round face, motioned for me to step in front of him. As I did, he grabbed my carry-on bag and said, "I'll carry that for you."

"It's okay," I said, startled, as I tried to hold onto my bag. He yanked the bag from my hand and walked by me, toward the exit.

"Wait a minute!" I said as I hurried after him, not sure if I should call for help. I saw him pause to look at the name tag on my bag then he turned and handed the bag to me and walked away.

A bit stunned, I followed the crowd toward the exit. The excitement I had about missionary work was dissipating, and I was truly leery of what was ahead. I felt there were elements at work that I didn't understand; that maybe someone was taking this a lot more seriously than I was. And that perhaps I was in some danger that I hadn't imagined or would ever understand. I took a deep breath and tried to shake off the strange string of events, now two in a row.

The mission board had told me that two workers from the school would meet me at the airport. I had no idea how I would find them but thought perhaps the missionary office in the States had sent them a photo of me. Nevertheless, I walked out onto the curbing just outside the airport doors and stood in a swarm of people and looked for any sign of the school staff.

Within seconds I noticed a man with a friendly face holding a sign with my name on it. Relieved, I smiled and walked quickly in his direction. When he saw me, he turned abruptly and walked away. Then a woman walked up to me.

"Ms. Palmer?"

I smiled and nodded.

"My name is Keiko. Welcome to Japan." She had a pleasant smile and kind eyes and dressed very much like a schoolteacher, in a violet-colored skirt and matching blouse. "Please follow me. We have a van waiting for you."

She walked next to me toward the van, saying very little.

As I walked away from the airport, I knew I was in for some sort of adventure, but I didn't quite know what to expect. My life would be in the hands of God.

Once inside the van, Keiko introduced me to Mr. Akimitsu, the man with the abrupt greeting, who was also our driver. Soon we were traveling on a Tokyo highway with darkness flanking both sides, reflecting the uncertainty I felt inside.

The night before leaving for Japan, Mama laid her hand on my head and prayed a very short prayer: "God go with you." I would hang onto those words as I left home in the US on my first trip to Asia. The memory of Mama's blessing would undergird me in the challenges ahead.

Over the years, I've learned that if God is not going along on that trail ahead, it's best not to go. It's critical to consult Him and to have His blessing on any new journey because He will provide the wisdom, protection, and guidance that is needed!

My favorite example of this is found in the book of Exodus. As the story goes, Moses is leading the Israelites toward Canaan, the promised land. It's a pretty big task and involves some danger, so Moses goes to God for reassurance. He says to God, "If your Presence does not go with us, do not send us up from here" (Exodus 33:15, NIV). Moses understood that there is safety in God's presence. "And the Lord said to Moses, 'I will do this very thing you have asked, for you have found favor in my sight, and I know you by name'" (Exodus 33:17, ISV).

* * * * * * *

If you are about to blaze a new trail, you may want to first verify that God is going with you. (I felt the Holy Spirit's attention on that.) Not every good idea is a God-idea, and it does matter immensely what He thinks.

Remember too that if God is sending you to the mission field, He will not let you fall as you trust Him and rely on Him. "For I am the Lord your God who takes hold of your right hand and says to you, 'Do not fear; I will help you'" (Isaiah 41:13, NIV).

Also, it is written: "For He shall give His angels charge over you, to keep you in all your ways" (Psalm 91:11, NKJV).

And as the psalmist says, "He will cover you with his feathers; under His wings you will find refuge; His faithfulness is a shield and rampart" (Psalm 91:4, NIV).

I would learn that firsthand during my stay in Japan.

3

Fuji

I had a seat facing south, which left me traveling backward when the Shinkansen bullet train pulled out of Osaka station for my first trip to Tokyo. Sometime within the hour, I must have dozed off, and when I woke, I was facing the window and my eyes rested on a little village, so delicate and beautiful all at once that it startled me!

It was like a make-believe world with little houses in straight lines, all boasting traditional Japanese green tiled roofs. The entire village must have only been a dozen miles across and in between the houses, I saw a handful of streets that all ended at the base of a mountain.

The mountain seemed to lean forward just a bit, like a canopy over a garden, and it was green, every inch, but not an ordinary green, a rich, deep, nearly sensual green. And the village was quiet, hardly a movement anywhere, except for an occasional car that seemed to nearly float down the street. And under the sun, everything glistened. Sparks of light darted off the windows of those small houses, and even off the grass on the ground, making it shimmy like sea water in sunlight.

The train passed the village in a matter of seconds, and I noticed twenty minutes or so later, that we'd pass another village, just as lovely as the first, and so it went for miles.

* * * * * * *

The heavens declare the glory of God; and the skies proclaim the work of his hands. (Psalm 19:1, NIV)

4

Kyoto

T he Japanese school campus where I taught Oral English was a "closed" community with a gated entrance. I seldom left the grounds during the week, mostly because I was too tired, but I looked forward to getting out on weekends.

I loved Kyoto, with its traditional architecture and bright colors. I'd take the thirty-minute train ride from Kobe to some of my favorite spots in the heart of Kyoto and walk along the narrow streets where I'd window shop or stop inside some quaint little bakery for traditional cake and tea.

On these outings, I always noticed that Japanese men seldom gave me a second glance. It was almost as if I didn't exist. The hand holding the hand of a Japanese man was a Japanese woman, and that was the standard. Their desire was for their own.

On occasion, I might find a white man with a Japanese woman, but never a Japanese man with a black woman or a black man with a Japanese woman. Nor did I find their features romantically attractive, except on occasion.

So dating was not something I did while there. However, one day, in the middle of the school semester, my nonexistent romantic life would take an unexpected turn, in the form of a handsome Irishman named Peter.

At first, the workday seemed rather ordinary. The entire school gathered in the campus auditorium for morning prayer and singing as usual. I arrived just in time for prayer and sat next to the other missionaries in the balcony. I had learned to sing in fluent Japanese and my Japanese vocabulary was becoming fairly good. We sang a few hymns then took our seats while Hiro sensei went to the podium for announcements.

To my surprise, she introduced a gospel band from Kyoto, a significant break from our traditional morning worship and prayer ceremony. I was glad for the change in routine and watched as three people filed onstage: two white men, and a black woman. I was so glad to see the black woman, and I couldn't help but stare at her wavy black hair and dark skin. It was a rare sighting in Japan, and I was eager to connect with anything familiar.

The band sang a few gospel songs and shortly after, we were dismissed to our classes. I didn't think much else of it, until later in the day when Hiro sensei invited me and the other missionary-teachers to have tea with the band. That wasn't unusual because the Japanese teachers loved to entertain and give presents. During tea, the group was introduced: Peter, the main signer, a tall, handsome Irishman; Bobby, the soft spoken and quiet guitar player; and Natasha, the black woman with the lovely voice.

Peter was friendly and outspoken. His reddish-brown hair and deep, warm voice were disarming, and he had a pleasant mouth. I liked him instantly.

Peter told us about his ministry in Japan. I found out that he migrated from Ireland to Japan to preach in the streets of Kyoto. As a street preacher, he would go to downtown neighborhoods spreading the gospel of Jesus and handing out hot meals of curry and rice from the back of a van. He and his band would sometimes sing and play music as part of their ministry.

Peter had become friendly with one of the missionary teachers and had managed to get himself invited to perform during one of our morning services at the school. That's how we ended up together at tea.

I didn't think much about Peter after that first meeting and introduction until I got a call from Natasha inviting me to one of their evangelism projects in the streets of downtown Kyoto. I agreed to go, and took Jane, one of the other missionaries, with me.

Jane had just joined the teaching staff at the school. She was a short white woman with beautiful black curly hair. She was also intensely self-defacing, often comparing herself to a cow. But she was funny and easy to be with, so we spent quite a lot of time together talking about our Japanese experience and reflecting on our homes back in the US.

There was only a handful of us, sometimes lonely missionaries, and so we stuck together and developed friendships quickly. International phone calls weren't as convenient as they are today, and certainly not cell phones. So we became confidants, counselor, surrogate parents, and stand-in sisters for each other.

Jane, being new to the missionary house on campus, I thought it would be good to have her go along with me to Kyoto, so we could both get off campus and have a little change of pace. She quickly agreed.

Late one afternoon, Peter and his team, Natasha and Barry, picked us up outside the train station in Kyoto in an old white van, and taxied us to one of the downtown neighborhoods. Within seconds of parking the van, Peter was outside talking to homeless people while Natasha and Barry began spooning out plates of curry and rice to men gathering around the back of the van.

Peter, speaking Japanese with an Irish accent, told the men about Jesus. He was so focused on what he was doing, as if nothing else mattered to him.

I stayed mainly at the back door of the van, with Jane and Natasha, helping to dish out plates of food.

Near the end of the evening, Peter walked over to me and uncurled his large fingers to reveal one thousand yen. "A homeless man gave this to me," he said. "They have so little, yet they are willing to give whatever they have."

Later that evening, at the close of the event, we joined hands to pray—me, Peter, Natasha, Jane, and Barry. Peter was standing across from me. As we bowed heads in prayer, Peter suddenly said, "Kawai." I opened my eyes to see him looking at me and smiling. I smiled, having no idea what he just said, until Jane explained that "Kawai" meant, "cute." I blushed and bowed my head in prayer. In my heart, I thought he was beautiful.

Shortly after that night, I got a call from Peter, personally this time, inviting me for a weekend prayer retreat with his band. They were all going to a retreat house in northern Japan. We only spoke for a few minutes, but it didn't take long to convince me. "Just a chance to hang out and pray," he said. I promised him I'd go.

That night I had a dream. Maybe because I was lonely for male company, for intimacy; I dreamt that Peter and I were married and had become a traveling missionary couple in Japan. He was like a church mouse, poor with nothing to offer me except his great love for Jesus.

In the dream, I saw us sleeping on the floor of an old house that a kind Japanese man let us use while we ministered in the area. I don't think it bothered Peter that we had to sleep on the floor. His eyes were full of dreams of being of service to God and he felt we had everything—our ministry to God and each other, and I felt the same. We only had a few pieces of clothes and had no idea how we'd get by from one day to the next, but none of that seemed to matter. Life and service to God overwhelmed and engulfed us. We both trusted God.

When I woke, I was surprised at how satisfying the dream was to me. I hardly knew Peter except for him sitting across from me at the table during tea that day after his performance at the school, and that one stint feeding the homeless. I thought maybe I was just lonely and that's why I dreamt about him, but it made me eager to see him again. I knew I'd find out during the weekend retreat whether there was some connection between us.

During the week leading up to the retreat, I ran into Jane, and as was customary, we talked about our plans for the weekend. I mentioned to her that I was planning to join Peter and the band at the prayer retreat. Her response surprised me.

She said that I was asking for trouble, that Peter was a renegade preacher not licensed by the Japanese government (I'm not sure how she knew that and now think that she made an assumption); and moreover, that I might get in trouble with the mission board that sent me to Japan.

My heart sank. *What if I lose my job?* The thought had never occurred to me before that moment.

Suddenly, I felt as if a spirit of fear settled over me. I didn't question the soundness of Jane's remarks because she had effectively managed to tap into one of my deepest fears—failing in Japan and getting sent back home, to my shame and the embarrassment of my family.

I felt I had better do what was expected of me by the mission board. As a black woman missionary who was born in Jamaica and not the US as the Japanese prefer, and not white, as the Japanese also prefer, I felt as if I was teetering on a precipice and had no room for error.

Living on campus, I always felt like I existed under a glass darkly. When I got my mail, it was usually opened. I never knew who opened my mail, nor did I ask. I was afraid to ask.

I was an oddball teaching at an elite school in a country where appearance and status was everything. I was young, and a babe in Christ, and easily feared their perceptions.

My fears would occasionally overshadow any success I had as a missionary and teacher: My students were making good progress in their studies, for example, performing well in speech competitions (one of them made it to the finals in Tokyo); and I was able to help lead Bible studies after classes, my little contribution as a missionary.

All this sometimes took a back seat to my own sense of insecurity of being a foreigner in a "closed" society. I was convinced that one misstep and the Japanese host and the mission board would find a reason to send me home. Losing my job in the middle of the semester would also mean losing my students, my apartment, and my livelihood. I wasn't prepared for that. Suddenly, a pleasant weekend prayer retreat took on heaviness, and seemed more like a threat than a blessing.

Back in my apartment, on the day I was scheduled to leave for northern Japan, I shut the door behind me. I watched the clock until I knew the train had left Kobe for its trek north—until I knew there was now no way to make it to the retreat in time.

In the hours that followed, I tried to convince myself that I had made the best logical decision; but really, I felt I blew it. *He will be waiting for me at the station.*

Peter didn't call to see why I didn't show up that day, and I didn't call him to explain. Maybe he was just as frightened as I was. In any case, we never spoke again.

Singles in the mission field face an extra set of challenges. For one thing, it can be lonely sometimes—there is so much to take in, so much to do, yet you are still a regular woman or man with feelings, hormones, and dreams like everyone else. Add to that the challenge of representing a mission board or church as their ambassador to the host country. There is a high level of responsibility and protocol which should rightfully be respected.

So where does romance fit in? At first, I thought Jane was an annoying voice of fear that caused me to wimp out and miss an opportunity to get to know Peter. But the Lord allowed me to see, as I was rethinking the event and writing this book, that Jane was right. Maybe she didn't know much about Peter and perhaps she made some wrong assumptions about him and his band being unregistered preaching renegades in Japan, but her conclusion was accurate. Going away with Peter, Natasha and Barry on a weekend prayer retreat would have been unwise. I was a bit naive and ready to trust them because they professed Christ, but I really didn't know enough about them.

The Bible says avoid even the appearance of evil (see 1 Thessalonians 5:22). I was starry eyed with thoughts of romance, and sincerely thought it would be a source of support and a reprieve from an otherwise stressful environment. Jane brought the voice of reason and helped me to re-focus.

As an ambassador for Christ, how one conducts oneself in a host country is crucial. It matters what they think. In the end, the goal is to be Christ-like and represent God well. To walk in honor and integrity. Dating should always be in a public place and the guy (or girl) should be respectful and bring honor to your name and your God.

Beyond the initial disappointment, Jane helped me to remember that I was a missionary first and foremost. I had a duty to the mission board, and I was on the job in Japan to share my faith and set a good example. And that I shouldn't do anything to jeopardize that rare gospel opportunity (I felt God's attention on this). In other words, when the missionary gets the opportunity to share the gospel, it is an incredibly important occasion, and should take priority over everything else because it could transform lives, and the opportunity might not come again for some of those people.

It was up to me to make sure no one misunderstood or misinterpreted any of my actions (I felt God's attention on this). The host country would have frowned on that "prayer retreat," especially my host friends on the school staff who felt it was their responsibility to watch over me.

What I should have required, and the respectable thing for Peter to do if he wanted to get to know me, would have been to meet in a public place for tea or dinner. That would leave little or no room for misunderstanding and scrutiny. This isn't even a culturally based approach, but simply good manners (I felt God's attention on this).

My first time wearing a kimono.

* * * * * * *

Did you take a step of faith in ministry and now find that it is a lot more challenging than you imagined? Give yourself credit for trying (I felt God's attention on this), as you do your best to honor God in the mission field.

And everywhere is a mission field. Now, let's move on to our next destination.

A Trailblazer's Journey to:
JAMAICA

5

Morant Bay

My grandmother, "Mama," is sitting on her favorite wooden bench on the veranda of her home—a modest three-room house with a leaky zinc roof. Her hair is tied with a faded handkerchief and her thick pepper-salt colored braids stick out around her ears in all directions.

Mama is about to pray. She stands facing the sunset, and as she opens her mouth and begins to speak, her words whirl upward to the top of the mango trees and into the Jamaican gully and even flows to the sun. "Jesus. Jesus. Yes, my Jesus. Thank you, Jesus."

The most mesmerizing part of the island is the part Mama stands on and fills with prayers each evening. When Mama prays, the land in front of her house seems to take on life, as if angels are present and dancing to the tone of her voice.

* * * * * * *

Often, when her daughters and grandchildren are present, she enjoys telling stories, carrying forward a rich heritage of oral traditions. Today, she is telling the story about her grandfather, the most honorable Paul Bogle, the Jamaican national hero.

"Dem say 'im come fram Scatland 'an 'im wife come fram Wes' Afrika. Whe-eva 'im go, evrybady know Paul Bogle." As Mama tells her story, the mango trees in front of the house sway in the breeze and light is pilfering through the branches, bringing specks of rainbow colors that fall across her shoulders.

In the middle of her story, her eyes daze over as if she's gone somewhere far away, perhaps to the docks in Kingston in the mid-1800s, watching from the eyes of her spirit as her grandparents meet for the first time.

Mama doesn't remember a lot about Paul Bogle's life, only that she is the granddaughter of the revolutionary who had a plantation in Morant Bay, Jamaica. He was from Scotland and he married a West African woman, who was most likely a product of slavery. Over the years, their lives were like the stormy weather on the island— their fragile marriage was challenged by wars on the high seas and British colonization.

On one dreaded day, in an attempt with other Jamaicans to assert his right as a landowner, Mr. Bogle clashed with the British authorities and quickly found himself in a bloody confrontation. As a deacon of the church, the turn of events was far from the intention of his heart, I imagine, but nevertheless, the consequences of his participation in the protest would be fatal—he was caught and hanged by the British.

The island has celebrated his courage ever since, placing his image on currency in memoriam. (Except the image is not of the Scottish Bogle because no one knew what he looked like at the time.)

Mama seems satisfied as she finishes her story and studies our faces, that despite the leaky zinc roof over our heads and the poverty that has plagued us, God has blessed us with a rich legacy.

When Mama wasn't spending herself working in the fields, she was reaching for inspiration—praying to Jesus with faith that could shake a mango tree or sharing pieces of our family history. So it was on those days after dinner as we sat together on the veranda.

* * * * * *

Blessed are the poor in spirit, for theirs is the kingdom of heaven.
Blessed are those who mourn, for they will be comforted.
Blessed are the meek, for they will inherit the earth.
Blessed are those who hunger and thirst for righteousness, for they will be filled.
Blessed are the merciful, for they will be shown mercy.
Blessed are the pure in heart, for they will see God.
Blessed are the peacemakers, for they will be called children of God.
Blessed are those who are persecuted because of righteousness, for theirs is the kingdom of heaven. (Matthew 5:3–10, NIV)

6

Sandy Corner

M ama is wearing one of her few good dresses. Her hair is combed and pinned down tight, and she has, wrapped in a handkerchief, a few coins which she intends to drop in the basket at church, her offering to God.

The ground is damp from rain the night before. As it often does in the tropical rain forest, it rains almost every night; and like the other mornings, as Mama steps off the veranda and unto the moist ground, she takes a deep breath and pulls in life, the crisp air, the sunshine, and the smell of fresh brewed coffee—the aroma still whirling upward from the kitchen.

This is Mama's day to worship God.

She steps one foot in front of the other as she walks past the family cemetery at the front of the house, down a steep hill, carefully now, not wanting to miss her step, and onto a strip of land called "Sandy Corner." Then, she makes her way up the road, slowing occasionally to say hello to a neighbor—Ms. Blanch in the small shack at the side of the road, and a Ms. Cloe whose house is perched on the small hill to her right.

Mama walks alone, tempered, determined, until she reaches a small church.

As she approaches the doors, she hears off-key singing escaping from the walls, which like everything else in Jamaica, is rich and warm and promising.

Mama smiles as she enters the church, and then finds a place to sit next to a window where she can stand and sing and worship Jesus. At the end of service, as Mama bows her head in prayer, the wind filters through the banana trees outside the church, swirl in through the windows, and mix with the sweat on her forehead.

She lifts her arms to Heaven and closes her eyes and finds herself in the presence of God! She is listening now, checking for the sweetness of His voice.

Her little shack with the leaky zinc roof sitting on the hillside seems a million miles away as she is wrapped in His re-assurance, and her heart surges with hope.

Outside the church, sounds of people praying rise above the roof-top and whirl past the mango trees and upward toward Heaven—the voice of the poor worshipping their God!

There's a cool breeze.

If you don't know Jesus as your Lord and savior, or if you'd like to renew your commitment to God, here's your chance! Simply say this prayer from the Billy Graham Evangelistic Association.

Prayer of Salvation

"Dear Lord Jesus, I know I am a sinner, and I ask for your forgiveness. I believe you died for my sins and rose from the dead. I trust and follow you as my Lord and Savior. Guide my life and help me to do your will. In your name, amen."[2]

A Trailblazer's Journey to:

THE UNITED STATES

The Transition

7

Genesis

Ahh. This chapter was a struggle. It was deleted more than once, and it is with some agony that I share this segment. I did not want to revisit the days of my freshman year in college. Here is why:

It was my second semester and I was registering for classes. I needed to choose an elective class and George, my advisor, told me to take an "easy A" class to balance off my more challenging courses. He suggested that I register for a course taught by a tenured teacher named Professor Songg.[3]

As I stood in line at registration, I had no idea that the course I was signing up for was an introduction to the occult. There was no mention of occult practices in the course description. The topic of the course itself had nothing to do with the occult. What happened next would be a total surprise to me and the other unsuspecting freshmen!

I would soon discover that Songg had his own hidden agenda of gurus, channeling spirits, psychic readings, and "past-life" regressions. Unbeknownst to the unwitting students that walked into his class that semester, he was on a mission to convert us to his way of thinking and being, to his occult practices. He would ignore the course description and with the sleight of hand, ease us into a world of confusion and darkness.

Until the day I registered for his class, I was relatively fearless and rooted in my Christian faith, but all that would change. For some of us, it would result in crashing our faith and putting our lives into a state of fear and confusion.

* * * * * * *

Professor Songg was a portly man with thinning grey hair and a kind face. He didn't have a syllabus like the other teachers and didn't require us to take notes or have a textbook. He emanated relaxation and talked about "oneness" and walking in love, and he taught that it was important to use daily affirmations to manifest tranquility and peace.

In every class, Songg transported us to his strange world of gurus, singing affirmations and past life regression. Still then in my teens, I had no idea the weight and impact of what Songg was teaching, what he was suggesting—that Jesus, my faith in God, and all I had learned was an illusion; and that I could in fact be my own god and forge my own destiny apart from Christ. He was mistaken in at least two significant ways (I felt God's attention on that). More on that later.

In my youth and ignorance, I believed Songg. It was college after all, a "safe" place, and the professors had the answers; they knew what they were talking about, and it wasn't my place to question them. At least, that's what I thought at the time.

With Songg's tutelage, by the middle of the semester I had a new vocabulary and heightened curiosity about the occult. I felt nurtured and had a sense of belonging to something interesting, not realizing the demonic undercurrent in Songg's teachings.

I was about to learn that there is a good reason why God tells us to avoid the occult—those experiences that lead away from Him.

* * * * * * *

One day, near the end of the semester, Songg invited some members of the class to a weekend retreat. He charged us a fee for the housing and meals and had intended the weekend as a chance to go further into the occult topics introduced in his class.

That weekend, several of us, including Songg, met in a private house that Songg rented, nestled in a thick pine forest in southern New England. The house was cozy and warm—the sort of place with hanging herbs, and cranberry smells in every room.

On the first day of the retreat, as we gathered in the living room for one of our sessions, I could tell by looking at everyone that they were all "free thinkers"—Songg, with his "forward" philosophy that we all create our own reality and determine our destiny apart from God; Herbie, a breatharian, who believed he could lead people into healthy spaces by coaxing them in deep breathing and imagery; and the rest of us who looked at them in awe.

We had meals together that weekend, and talked about New Age stuff, like channeling spirits, automatic writing and psychic readings.

There was something resembling "unconditional love" emanating from the leaders of the group, but it also felt seductive. Herbie stroked my arm as he passed by, for example, and everyone gave hugs.

The encounter was sensual and platonic at the same time. I wasn't from a culture of outward affection and during those early college years, I didn't have a point of comparison to determine what healthy outward affection looked like. It didn't occur to me that what was happening was inappropriate at least. I trusted them, and it was a bad setup for what came next.

One cool evening that weekend, Songg determined that we should a have a ritual. It may have been sometime after dinner, as we sat talking, when he looked at me and asked, "How would you like to be a princess?" I never questioned his character or authority and quickly agreed to an ancient ritual of welcoming the moon.

Herbie scribbled out a prayer on a piece of paper that I would repeat during the ritual and the next thing I knew, I was in a procession to a nearby lake with Songg and the others for the ancient worship ceremony.

During the ritual, I was to pretend to be a goddess. I didn't know the goddess, had never thought about the goddess, and didn't even think the goddess was real. It just seemed like a fun thing to do, and I was thrilled that we were all getting so into it.

I found the following paragraphs in my journal recently, regarding that harrowing night. I wrote it in the spring of my freshman year in college. I refrained from editing (except names). I was nineteen.

Last night we performed a ritual where as I was to be a priestess and Herbie[4] was the priest and we, along with the group, were to welcome the moon and crossing of the planets which occurs every 2000 years.

I was told that I would have welcome them into an imaginary circle which Herbie would construct. Its a welcoming method, while walking in the woods, I got the idea to pick wild flowers and hand them to each person as they enter the circle (little did I know that the flowers I chose were narcissus which were traditionally used by the brides in pagan rituals to give to their husbands to represent peace and love.)

I was dressed in a white robe a towel for a veil and a sheet for a stroll. With much anticipation, I was taken to the ritual grounds.

The scenery consisted of a gigantic old oak tree that had lost all its leaves, with the moon setting directly over it, also a large iron bin in front of it, filled with blazing wood.

After Herbie prepared the circle, he was to signify which side was the north entrance and I was to stand in that area. By chance, when he came over to stage me, I was already there.

I welcomed each person with a kiss and a narcisus and peace. I read the invocation which stated that "I am the moon goddess, sorceress of the great abyss." The goddesses message was that everyone should love each other and live in peace.

I then threw a bad thought into the fire (which we wrote earlier) and repeated the words OAM, then the good thoughts were thrown in that we wanted to secure, and oam followed. I kissed and told everyone I love them. We hugged, and my energy increased 300 degrees.

We ended it; and I went back feeling overly charged, anxious, strange because I enjoyed the ritual and felt comfortable with it, and frightened because I didn't understand what it all meant, and angry because everyone went to sleep, and I had no one physically that I could talk to.

Songg continued his indoctrination during the college under-graduate years that followed. "Just register for anything in my department," he'd tell me. Regardless of what was written in the course catalog, Songg would ignore the course description and use the opportunity to bring more of the same occult experience. With his guidance, I was beginning to disconnect from my faith in God, and identify with a cosmic, formless, ambiguous entity that Songg referred to as the "Universe."

* * * * * * *

I found the experience totally consuming, but one day, in the midst of the confusion, I came across a healthy distraction in the form of a handsome Italian named Carter.

It happened when I was walking to class. I saw Carter walking in the opposite direction with a mutual friend, Ronnie.

Ronnie introduced us, then walked off and left us standing there, staring at each other. After some small talk, none of which I remember now, Carter startled me by reaching for my hand, lifting it to his lips, and kissing it. The kiss was followed by a request for a date.

If there were other people walking by at that moment, I didn't notice them. I was totally mesmerized by him. It was his gentle green eyes and silky black hair, cut in a wiffle. I had bushy unmanageable hair, full lips and dimples.

As much as I looked forward to going on that date with Carter, I was hesitant to get involved with anyone. In my last relationship the guy I was dating chose the other girl. I didn't want to risk another heartbreak.

On date night I struggled with whether to meet Carter. It was literally a last-minute decision when I headed for the door.

* * * * * * *

Our date was at Horseneck Beach. To my surprise, Carter was the easiest person in the world to be with, and after seconds, I felt as if I had known him all my life. We walked the long strip of sandy beach in the dark and talked about our dreams and about our classes at the university. Then, we sat on a sand dune, cuddled and waited for the sun to rise.

Before long, we were spending almost every day together. I loved being with him because he was a refreshing distraction from the Songg effect and all the confusion I felt bubbling up from the New Age Movement. He would often sing to me, some sweet off-tune melody by Prince or an "oldie." And we spent lots of time at the beach, holding hands and talking about our dreams for the future. By the end of summer, Carter was off with the Marines to Okinawa, Japan. We spoke regularly on the phone about building a life together once he returned to the US.

While Carter was away in the military, I got a job as Songg's work study student. I still had faith in Songg as a mentor and in truth, he seemed quite sincere about his tutelage, however misguided at the time.

My job was to show up at Songg's office and create a file system for all his books on the New Age movement. I learned about his guru, a black man in India with the large afro, and spent many hours leafing through his books on the occult.

By now, I was in my early twenties and thought that all the issues I had in the New Age Movement was just growing pains and that if I stayed with it, I'd become good at fortune telling, past life regressions, astral projections, etc.

Despite the confusion and loneliness stemming from the New Age Movement, I still respected Songg and felt he was leading me to a better understanding of the world. But one event would open my eyes—one event that made me wish I could turn back time.

It was a cool summer morning when Songg introduced me to a woman that visited his office, named Shandra. I thought nothing of the introduction until he turned to me and said, "Shandra does channeling, automatic writing." My eyes lit up. I had never met a person who was an actual channel and thought that if I could channel, it would open a world of answers for me.

The professor left the room and left us ladies alone to chat.

"How do you do it?" I asked.

"I just sit and get quiet and let the spirit write through me. It's easy." She said, "I'll teach you."

A pretty white girl, twenties, with a gentle smile and white teeth, she spoke eagerly as I listened and soaked it all in. I could tell we were from different worlds: me with my East Indian, West African, Scottish, and Chinese ancestry; and her with her European features—bone straight brown hair, and olive complexion. But we both longed for power, craved answers.

I listened intently as she described the process, not understanding the weight of what she was suggesting.

At that moment, I was far from Jesus. I mean, I prayed, but didn't rely on Him as my personal savior. I didn't know what the Bible said about channeling. I was convinced that Songg was right and sincerely thought I was on the right road to success and fulfillment.

Shandra was confident, even radiant! She soon had me convinced that the vacuum I felt, this sense that there was something more, was hidden in the supernatural world of channeling. I decided that day while sitting there listening to her blissful quiet voice, that I would give it a try. The longer she spoke, the more my doubts, the few I had, vanished and I was ready to step into the unknown.

The evening following my meeting with Shandra, I went back to my dorm room and sat quietly at my desk.

After a pensive moment, I felt a check in my spirit and a flood of feelings I couldn't sort out—some fear about what might happen. *What is this I'm doing?* The feelings factored in the memories of Jamaica, all the ghost stories and all the spookiness I had heard about the spirit realm.

I hesitated again as I wondered who would come through when I channeled. *Should I call on someone specific? Should I just see who comes?* Finally, I decided to wing it. Throwing caution aside, I began! I grabbed a piece of paper and reached for a pen and sat silently.

* * * * * * *

The sum of all the occult activity—the channeling, the psychic readings, Tarot Cards, Book of Ruins, and other New Age vices left me feeling addicted to the process and tired. The process was time consuming and endless. I carried Tarot Cards with me, for example, and consulted them during the day. It became difficult to make simple decisions because I developed a fear of being wrong, a fear of the unknown, and a fear of the future. The curious, and relatively clear-headed personality I had on that first day as a college freshman was replaced with decision paralysis and insecurity.

In the middle of it all, I got a call from Carter from his base in Okinawa. I wished more than anything that we could be together, that I could return to that sense of normalcy that I felt when we walked the beach, went to the mall for ice cream, or travelled the ferry to Cape Cod, but that was in the past. Some weeks after our conversation, I got this letter from him:

> How do? Me do, do. I'm K. Just chillin' here at work, literally. Missin' you sweety pie, I got your letters & pictures. I told you how much I'm in love with the pictures and the letters were sweet. I'm glad you decided to send them. I'm sorry you feel so uptight, like your world is shaking. How come cutie? I know you want to wait til'

we're together, but we (I) can't wait. Something is tearing you up and it's boogin'… me baby.

I also know that you want 2 come soon, [to Okinawa] but it can't be done for a while yet. I want 2 CU 2 cutie, ya know? I hope you do. Just save $ and if I can get leave I'll call you and say, "Pack your bags baby!" Your flight leaves in 2 weeks. Got it. Save, save, save…send me more pictures. I love you, your so beautiful…send me kisses and hugs.

I never got a chance to tell Carter about all the chaos that was springing from Songg's classes. In the middle of all the confusion and poor choices, coupled with the distance between us, we eventually drifted apart.

By delving into the occult, I was seeking a strong voice; I was a teenager looking for direction. I was convinced by the occult, by Songg, that if I took of the "fruit" (channeling, tarot cards, etc.), it would make me more like God—wise and confident. But I had it all backwards. I couldn't be more like God apart from God. The occult activity only served to drive a rift between God and me.

There is a good reason why God gives this warning:

> There shall not be found among you any-one…who practices witchcraft, or a soothsayer, or one who interprets omens, or a sorcerer, or one who conjures spells, or a medium, or a spir-itist, or one who calls up the dead. For all who do these things are an abomination to the LORD, and because of these abominations the LORD your God drives them out from before you. You

shall be blameless before the Lord your God. (Deuteronomy 18:10–12, NKJV)

Ouija Boards, tarot cards, psychics, astral projections, etc., are the Venus Fly Trap of the underworld. It only guarantees destruction, waste of time, and loss. It is a fear-based system: fear of the future, fear of failing, fear of not knowing. It is ethereal, undefined, and narcissistic. It's a sad (though sometimes sincere) attempt at finding answers and satisfaction in life that only leads to more confusion and uncertainty.

I would eventually realize that what Songg offered me—the vague, foul, tricky and narcissistic occult world—was enormously inferior to what I would gain in Christ Jesus.

Life in Jesus is one of precision and excellence! It is faith-based, not fear-based. God brings true answers, light into every situation, and true guidance (I felt the Holy Spirit's attention on that). He builds faith, healthy thinking, prayer, and incredible hope in those who trust in Him! (See Jeremiah 29:11.)

In contrast, the devil uses lies, fear, and deception to suppress and distort lives—his intentions being to kill, steal, and destroy. (See John 10:10.) He wants to steal peace, destroy confidence, and keep a person in a state of constant worry, anxiety, and self-obsession. That is the culture of the occult world.

* * * * * * *

God is ready to forgive and restore the lives of anyone who has practiced the occult, and through repentance and the cleansing blood of Christ, you become a new creation. "Therefore if anyone *is* in Christ, *he* is a new creation; old things are passed away, behold, all things are become new" (2 Corinthians 5:17, NKJV). You get a fresh start with God, and your past no longer dictates your future.

So once I accepted Jesus as Lord, I started having these amazing and incredible visions of what I could become, and it didn't involve fear or paying some woman with a dark mind to read my palm. It didn't involve staring at a picture of a guru with a big afro to gain "enlightenment," or living in the past.

It involved impacting my world with the gospel of Jesus Christ and bringing hope. By the grace of God, I became part of the solution and not part of the problem. My life took on different meaning. It became less about me and more about how I might serve humanity.

I couldn't get my mind around the benefits of being a Christian until I stepped into it. At first, I thought it meant becoming "religious" and stepping into a boring, colorless, unchallenging, and unappealing life locked in by church customs and traditions. And indeed, I stumbled upon some churches that were like that.

But then I came to realize that Jesus didn't die so that I could find a religion. He died that I might find the Kingdom! I would learn that He is ruler of the incredible Kingdom of God and that the future He offers is all at once dynamic, colorful, and pleasant; one that challenges me to live a life that is expansive. It's nothing like I had imagined. The true "church" of Christ is amazing!

God is about rebuilding, about freeing and restoring lives. His goal is real impact (see Revelation 3) and real power (I felt the Holy Spirit's attention on that). He is God of action, of change, of innovation! He is incredibly forward thinking and enormously effective, and you can always rely on His word. (See Isaiah 55:11.)

Considering all this, why would I settle for a Ouija board or tarot card experience when I can partner with God to change and impact my world? God is obviously a superior choice, but I didn't know that as a college freshman!

When I got involved in the New Age Movement, I was shy and had trouble expressing myself. I was young and deceived into thinking I had found the right path to power and self-expression.

It was like blazing a trail into a broken forest. By the grace and power of God, by the authority of the name of Jesus, and by the power of the Holy Spirit (I felt the Holy Spirit's attention on that), I would finally, after many years, sever ties to the New Age Movement—and break free from the occult.

I would repent, recant, dismiss and cancel the invocation I spoke during the ceremony at the weekend retreat. Now, I am careful to avoid all trails that lead into the occult! I've learned to choose life, to courageously reach out and take the hand of God.

* * * * * *

If you've been pulled off into the occult, it's not too late to turn your life around. Give Jesus a chance to show you a glimpse of what you can become with Him by your side! Scripture gives an example of believers who quit the occult!

> And many who believed came confessing and telling their deeds. Also, many of those who practiced magic brought their books together and burned *them* in the sight of all. And they counted up the value of them, and *it* totaled fifty thousand pieces of silver. So the word of the Lord grew mightily and prevailed. (Acts 19:18–20, NKJV)

It took me years to fully commit to God, to realize what I'm telling you now. Life with God is about relationship. Trust develops over time.

The following chapters will show my struggle and demonstrate God's faithfulness. Hopefully you will see from these stories that no matter what you've done or how far off track you've gotten, God is there for you with outstretched hands.

His plans for you are good and not evil. To give you a future and a hope. (See Jeremiah 29:11.)

8

Firewalk in Vermont

Disclaimer: This chapter is about a firewalk experience. Firewalks are inherently dangerous and can cause serious injuries. Do not try this at home!

I was an insecure young college student searching for personal power when I signed up for a firewalk workshop led by the famed motivational speaker, M. T. Valentino.[5]

By this time, in my early twenties, I was at a crossroad. I was reaching for Jesus and had recently prayed the prayer of salvation and wanted to allow God to lead my life, but I was trapped by old habits—I still checked the Book of Ruins and Tarot Cards in between reading my Bible, for example.

I didn't understand the power of Jesus in my life at the time and was still trying to work out my own deliverance. I didn't belong to a good church, so I wasn't getting any helpful guidance. So when I heard about the firewalk workshop I thought it might be the answer, or at least part of the answer to personal power, to being free from fear. That's how I ended up in the hills of Vermont one fall day, standing before a bed of hot coals, preparing to walk on fire!

* * * * * * *

I found an entry in my journal about the firewalk experience and my thoughts about surrendering to Jesus. The journal entry opens at the firewalk workshop. I am next in line, standing before a ten-foot bed of hot coals.

During the firewalk, because I was so nervous, the workshop leader walked along side, he on the grass, me on the hot coals, and he gripped my forearm to guide me across; but the biggest challenge he faced was getting me to take the first step as I stood terrified in front of the hot coals.

My journal entry, written more than twenty years ago, picks up at the point where I am standing in front of the hot coals, frozen in fear, while the workshop leader is tirelessly coaxing me into the right state of mind by reassuring me and having me (and the crowd around me) repeat certain words:

> "As I take the first step."
>
> "As I take the first step," I repeated.
>
> "My body will do," he continued, "whatever it needs to do to protect itself." We repeated those words over and over at his command. The crowd gathered in tightly around the ten-foot bed of hot coals—eyes peering at the small framed woman at the front of the line. I straightened my shoulders and looked up. I felt courage come and go like hot flashes.
>
> "I can't," I whimpered.
>
> "Yes, you can!" snapped the workshop leader. Look up...get ready... Okay. Now." I froze. He tried again. "Repeat after me," he insisted.
>
> "As I take the first step..." I repeated word for word. I can't fail. I fail so much. I can't fail this too.
>
> The crowd fell into silence, or so it seemed. I looked up. The sky was illuminated by stars sitting in every place. Galaxies seemed to be watching me as I pushed my shoulders back as far as

I possibly could and led my small frame… the first step…the hot coals seemed cold under my right foot, as I quickly swung my other foot onto the coals and, head still looking upward, I walked quickly and carefully over the coals.

The large hands of the workshop leader gripped tightly around my forearm. Strange. For a moment there seemed to be silence. The crowd seemed gone. I no longer felt the workshop leader's grip—as if all stood still—no flickering lights in the sky—no coals—nothing. Hands grabbed my legs and some my shoulder, and I was whirled up toward the sky.

"You did it," shouted the enthusiastic crowd on the other side, sharing in my firewalk victory. Somehow, being swung overhead by the strangers/co-victory partners seemed appropriate and I broke out a smile. I was ready to go again.

"Repeat after me," said the Reverend. "Jesus I invite you into my heart, take my life and work your will. I repent of my sins…" I said the words. I felt that same surge I did after the firewalk—victory stood near. Victory over decisions, nightmares and other things I wouldn't mention.

There were no crowds like at the firewalk, and even the preacher wasn't really there, as I watched his face shift from Camera 1 to Camera 2 on my TV set. I didn't hear any cheering of the crowd—it felt more like the silence I felt when stepping on the hot coals. But if the firewalk brought me surges of courage, then accepting Jesus would send me soaring, right? Well the two can't be compared—not fairly—one is temporary, one is eternal. The hot coals didn't hurt my feet—not even a blister, but God promised greater, lasting power.

The fireplace crackled in the sitting room as I lit dry leaves among the wood. Somehow, somewhere in me is the silence of this winter day—I know following Christ wouldn't be easy. It's like walking on an endless bed of hot coals—everything seems to oppose every step. But when I get to the other side, what a party we'll have. Me, Jesus, and every angel that knows to shout and celebrate. It may not be tomorrow certainly it's not today—but I'll reach the other side of my fiery trials and no one will shout louder than me—except maybe Jesus who walks alongside me, his hand gripping firmly around my forearm.

As I drove home from the firewalk, it seemed as if indeed, I had found some new inner strength, but it would be short lived. The "power" I thought I had gained wore off as the memory of the firewalk began to fade. Walking on fire was an ambitious and courageous attempt to free myself from my own limitations, but I needed more. In my young mind, I was beginning to understand that if I were to find lasting power, it would be at the foot of the cross. By the power of God. In the name of Jesus!

I laughed when I re-read that journal entry. "I know following Christ wouldn't be easy." I had written, "It's like walking on an endless bed of hot coals…" I have to say, sometimes it feels that way, but more oft than not, it does not.

In truth, Jesus takes a lot of the "heat"! He takes a lot of the blows that belong to me; He bears a lot of the burden. Praise God! Thank you, Jesus!

His love is so immense that He takes on more than we can imagine, more than we could handle, even the penalty for our sins—

death on a cross. Jesus died on a cross so that our lives could continue, so that we might live!

Honestly, I could have easily been consumed by what I saw in the occult—I only touched on a portion of it in this book. I believe that it was the prayers of friends and family, and the love and power of Jesus that saw me through. While I wandered off into the occult, God never took His eyes off me. He never lost track of where I was, and even in the darkest places, He held onto hope that one day I would be sitting here writing this book and trying to inspire others, to remind others that God is for them and wants them well!

Perhaps you think it's too late, or you're on the fence about surrendering your life to God! Let me assure you, whatever you're going through, He can handle it! It's hard to explain, even with a large reservoir of words, just how loving He is and how tremendously He cares. He stayed with me during the crazy occult experience and saw me to the other side as a statement of that great love.

It takes trusting Him.

Whatever you're going though, He's powerful to deliver. He is strong in a storm—and will help you if you let Him. If you don't know Jesus as your Lord and Savior, if you've never said the "sinner's prayer," then here is your chance. Simply say this prayer from the Billy Graham Evangelistic Association.

Prayer of Salvation

"Dear Lord Jesus, I know I am a sinner, and I ask for your forgiveness. I believe you died for my sins and rose from the dead. I trust and follow you as my Lord and Savior. Guide my life and help me to do your will. In your name, amen."[6]

Jesus says, "Behold, I stand at the door and knock. If anyone hears My voice and opens the door, I will come in to him and dine with him, and he with Me" (Revelations 3:20, NKJV).

If you read to the end of this book, you'll see that there is something about accepting Jesus as Savior that triggers another layer of existence (I felt the Holy Spirit's attention on this), where you live above gimmicks and walk in the strength of God. It starts with saying "Yes," to Jesus. That decision will massively change your life. (I feel the Holy Spirit's attention on this.)

9

Jesus at the Altar

I bashfully stepped through the doorway of a Baptist church in the small New England town.

I was tired.

I had been in the occult/New Age Movement for years. I was in my late twenties, but I felt like an old woman trapped in a house riddled with domestic abuse—the abuse was the sum of all I had experienced in the New Age Movement—intense confusion seeping out of channeling, automatic writing, and tarot card readings. I felt the occult practices had a grip on my life and was dragging me under.

I felt like I was going too fast in dangerous waters, as if my life was locked in by a perfect storm and I was about to capsize. One nineteenth-century writer says it best:

> The sun now being on the decline the days shortened…we met a very severe gale of wind and high seas and shipped a great deal of water in the space of ten hours. This made us work exceedingly hard at all our pumps a whole day; and one sea, which struck the ship with more force than any thing I ever met with of the kind before, laid her under water for some time, so that we thought she would have gone down.[7]

I found a seat somewhere near the back of the church and waited for the preacher to finish his sermon and issue the "call of salvation." I don't remember now what was preached, only that the portly black man with the kind face went on at length about something. Finally, he called for someone, anyone at all who might be "here today who does not know Christ." I picked myself up and wearily walked toward the altar, my silent steps occasionally interrupted by an "amen" springing from a man or woman in the pew. Finally, I reached the altar and stood alone in front of the preacher.

"Do you accept Jesus as your Lord and Savior?" he asked. The tiredness showing through my soul was from trouble sleeping and feeling like some of the bad choices I had made were refusing to release me. When I laid down to sleep at night, hoping for rest, I found that the darkness was there too, like I was lost in some sort of unfriendly forest. I would have nightmares about being chased and hunted, and sometimes, upon waking, I felt a clear sense of brokenness.

> Suffering much by villains in the late cause and being much concerned about the state of my soul…brought me very low; so that I became a burden to myself and viewed all things around me as emptiness and vanity, which could give no satisfaction to a troubled conscience.[8]

It was time to say "yes" to Jesus. I would say "yes," and mean it this time. I would not say "yes," and then go back to the occult practices, book of ruins, and tarot cards as I had done before. I would finally say "yes," and mean "yes," and stop heaping up trouble for myself by oscillating between the two worlds.

I had great hopes of what my life would be like when I said "yes" to Jesus. I saw the nightmares ending, and normalcy returning to my life. I wanted peace and to visit with friends, marry, and laugh again out loud and be at rest. It was how I had imagined my life would be when I started college, before the occult. Now, standing there at the altar, I sensed a storm raging but understood, or hoped at least, that Jesus would save me.

I needed Him to put things back together again. I needed someone more aggressive than the danger I was in to take the job of my deliverance.

"Yes," I answered the preacher, "I accept Jesus as my Lord and Savior."

> [The] ship was in such a shocking condition that we all thought she would instantly go down, and every one ran for their lives…but our lieutenant being the aggressor, he never quitted the ship…And by using every possible means, particularly frapping her together with many hawsers, and putting a great quantity of tallow below water where she was damaged, she was kept together: but it was well we did not meet with any gales of wind…[9]

Jesus, the "Aggressor" faced my trouble as I stood at the altar. It was as if He reached down from Heaven and kept me from "sinking." I became born again (I felt the Holy Sprit's attention on that).

From then on, I had an increasing sense of security against all "wind" and "gale." I found hope. I started to learn that there was someone stronger than all my struggles, and He would keep my life from "sinking."

This chapter describes a brief period of time—a moment of shifting from the occult world to a life of faith. Anyone who goes through a major life change experiences that initial sense of insecurity and loss to some degree. It's part of the human experience. But I thank God that those tough times didn't last. In my case, Jesus was incredibly helpful in causing me to transition out of it. (I felt the

Holy Spirit's attention on that). He brought hope and stability and a new sense of purpose to my life. Peace became my birthright.

Jesus is famous for running tough rescues, and He is extraordinarily good at it! Fortunate for us, He's not intimidated by the storms! And those He rescues He places under the protective authority of the Kingdom of God. As it states in the Bible:

> But now in Christ Jesus you who once were far away have been brought near by the blood of Christ. For he himself is our peace...For through him we both have access to the Father by one Spirit. Consequently, you are no longer foreigners and strangers, but fellow citizens with God's people and also members of his household. (Ephesians 2:13–19, NIV)

If you don't know Jesus as your Lord and savior, or if you'd like to renew your commitment to God, here's your chance! Just say, "Jesus, I surrender my life to you! Forgive me for my sins. I believe that you died for my sins and was raised from the dead. I accept you as my Lord and Savior. Come into my heart. Please help me!" And He will.

He really, really cares about you, and he is ready to forgive you and restore your life! He has you on His mind. It's not too late for you to say "Yes" to Jesus!

Accepting Jesus as Lord doesn't mean you will never again struggle. It means you will have a "Captain" on hand who understands how to handle all the "stormy seas" of life!

* * * * * * *

Over time, my new commitment to Christ, my new faith, would strengthen me in a way that I didn't know was possible, and launch a wonderful time of healing. Mostly, it would set me on a course for a healthy relationship with God.

THE UNITED STATES

Healing Moments

10

Newport by the Sea

Once upon a time, there was a town called Newport. And in that town were many mansions—white ones, blue ones, red tall brick ones, sitting on a cliff, overlooking the sea. And in front of those mansions ran a long windy dusty road for miles and miles and miles.

And so it was on my journey through Newport that I happened upon this place by the cliffs, and adorned with my summer hat, began a stroll along that dusty path.

And as I walked, I could see the ocean at the base of the cliff crashing over the rocks, and I could see too, the mansions and the many stories they could tell. Blue shutters, a gazebo, a flock of seagulls in blue sky—it made me want to stop and listen, and so I did, at the stories that filled the air and blew through the branches of bowed trees.

Now, the first mansion, as it were, just yards in front of me, hemmed in by large hedges and a wire fence. I stopped to stare at the windows near the roofline and wondered about the stories they might tell. I imagined the eyes through the centuries that looked through that window there on the left, admiring the sea crashing over the rocks at the base of the cliff perhaps. And I wondered too about the parties on the manicured front lawn—how those might have been.

I could see, in my imagination, belles in splendid laced gowns in hues of blue and scarlet, being twirled about in the arms of slender gentlemen as a live orchestra played Mozart in the gazebo nearby. So, I found myself smiling.

Then I pulled myself away and turned and looked again at the sea. For miles I could see the other half of Newport perched on the opposite shore; a quiet little place like this one. But what delighted me more than these were the cliffs themselves and the waves that hurled itself so boldly across the rocks.

And it was silent. As I walked along, I was delighted to find that I was suddenly alone. The mansions were hidden by tall prickly hedges, and for yards before me and yards behind me, I could see only empty paths and a few bowed trees.

As if taking a cue from my soul, I slowed my pace and breathed in as much of the fresh salty air as I could comfortably fit in one breath. *This is what I have been waiting for.* Solitude. It was quiet. "Father," I said, breaking the silence with my whispers, somehow feeling as if He too had paused and was standing there next to me.

I knew in that moment on that little path that wound along the edge of the cliffs, that path that skirted so many kingly estates, that God was somehow present, and I wondered if perhaps He was walking beside me. "Thank you for bringing me back here," I said. By "here," I meant this place where He and I were once again alone and at peace, like friends in a secret garden.

"Here," also meant to the edge of the Atlantic, which has been a source of unspeakable comfort for me always. Finally, "here," meant the cliffs, for it seemed to me that I had been there some years ago, a vague memory of a narrow path and mansions flicker across my mind, but so long ago, it took the feel of a dream.

What can I say to Him in this moment before I am flanked on all sides by pedestrians? "Thank you for being a great Father and a great Friend," I said, wishing I could reach out and take His hand. Then, the oddest thing happened. A familiar song filled my thoughts suddenly. "You are so beautiful, to Me." I smiled and walked along silently. Yes, indeed, He was near.

I walked on for a mile or more until I came to an imposing red brick mansion that seemed too large for one family or even ten. How could they possibly fill all the rooms? I imagined how I would manage such an estate. I would live in that section to the right, and there would be a garden just outside my window filled with yellow roses and a view of the sea.

Once upon a time, there was a place called Newport, and in that place, on a long dusty path that went for miles and miles and miles, adorned in my summer hat, I went walking. And on that walk, near two or three bowed trees, in the coolness of the day, I felt the presence of the King. "Father," I said, breaking the silence with my whispers.

A feather is taken by the wind, and the ocean is rolling in toward the shore.

My greatest fortune has been knowing God as Father and King and our many walks together. When I forget my way, I can always find Him by the sea.

As He has promised, "You will seek me and find me when you seek me with all your heart" (Jeremiah 29:11, NIV).

11

The Secret Garden

I sat alone
on a beach,
somewhere near the Japanese
Inland Sea,
and looked up,
searching
for You,
and found You,
flowing in the breeze,
You arrived.
God of my fathers,
how splendid
are Your thoughts
toward me.

The King

If [you] take
the wings of the morning
and dwell in the uttermost parts
of the sea,
even there
My hand will lead [you],
and My right hand
shall hold [you].

—Psalm 139:9–10

I found
a blossoming
tree
in the middle
of a Cape Cod beach
side forest
and was so impressed
by the thing,
that a smile
sprung
from me
and
I felt too
in the wind,
swirling,
unexpected,
the soft whisper
of the King.
"My Lord," I said.

The King

"…I have loved you
with an everlasting
love…
With unfailing love
I have drawn you
to Myself."

—Jeremiah 31:3, NLT

THE UNITED STATES

STATES

Weathering the Storms

12

New York

MURTAGH: I just witnessed a plane that appeared to be cruising at slightly lower-than-normal altitude over New York City, and it appears to have crashed into—I don't know which tower it is—but it hit directly in the middle of one of the World Trade Center Towers.
Lin: Sean, what kind of plane was it? Was it a small plane, a jet?
MURTAGH: It was a jet. It looked like a
two engine jet, maybe a 737."
—CNN transcript 9/11/01, 08:48 ET[10]

It's difficult to revisit that day. I was in my classroom working through a math problem with my algebra students when a woman swung open the door and gestured for me to come out and speak with her. *Maybe she has a message for one of my students.* At the doorway, she seemed flustered.

"You need to evacuate the classroom," she said. Seeing the puzzled look on my face, she continued, "All I know is that a plane flew into a building in New York. They're telling us to evacuate all government buildings!" Then, she hurried down the hallway.

I turned on my heels and walked quickly to the front of the class. "Guys, we need to stop here for today!" The students looked elated, then confused. I told them what little I knew and waited for them to leave the room; then I joined the procession of students flowing from neighboring classes, heading for the stairs.

I went directly home and turned on the television. What I saw sent chills through me—instant replays of a massive jet liner plowing into the side of one of the Twin Towers, with smoke, debris, chaos, confusion, screams filling the air! Then, a second plane hitting Tower 2! All I could do was stare at the horror flowing from the TV screen. Then, just outside my apartment, I heard someone screaming! I ran to the window and saw a middle-aged white woman running down the street, sobbing uncontrollably. Her cries tapered off as she ran inside a neighbor's home. I gathered that she had a loved one trapped in one of those buildings!

I felt incredibly helpless and overwhelmed as I tried to get my mind around what was happening. The news broadcasters were beginning to say that it may have been a terrorist attack that set both towers ablaze!

Several minutes into watching the instant replays, I needed to catch my breath, so I picked up my pet, Simba, and went outside. I sat on my lawn chair in the sun and looked up at the sky. The same sky that stretched above my home in Massachusetts, the calm sky, also formed a canopy over New York City; but there, it was filled with smoke, debris, and chaos!

The trouble in New York seemed too massive for my prayers—but I prayed anyway—for the people jumping from the burning and imploding buildings, for the families worried about their loved ones at ground zero. For a moment, life took on a strange tone—it felt surreal. Things like this didn't happen *here*. This sort of madness happened in other countries, not this one. But it *was* happening in this one.

In the middle of the storm and uncertainty, I needed to connect with something that I could rely on. I needed God. I needed His reassuring voice.

About six years prior to that stunning and terrible day, I learned firsthand how critical it is to have a relationship with God *before* disaster hits! I was a teacher in Japan traveling alone from Osaka to Tokyo when I was nearly kidnapped. It happened when I got off the train at a deserted station in the middle of the night to find a hotel. There were no taxis running at that hour, and in a moment of bad judgment, I agreed to take a ride to a hotel from two strangers that I met at the station.

During the journey, as I sat in the back of the car, I had a shocking revelation! God opened my understanding and I immediately understood that the driver and his female companion were predators! I suddenly knew that I needed to flee the vehicle and run for my life! When the car finally stopped, as I attempted to run, the driver reached back and tried to grab me! Fortunately for me, I had enough momentum to get out the car and run to safety!

My prayer during that ordeal was, "Jesus, help me!" And He did by keeping me calm and helping me to develop a plan of escape and execute it!

I know that if it were not for God showing up in the car that day, I may have been killed! My relationship with God saved my life!

After seeing the 9/11 broadcast, I ran to Him yet again, this time asking Him, even in my silence as I looked up at the sky, to calm my heart and reassure me of His presence and to help those in New York City.

The Bible tells us that the world as we know it will continue to deteriorate until Christ returns. (See 1 Timothy 3:1–5.) The best thing we can have in our toolbox for survival is a solid relationship with God. He does love us, and cares more than we can think or imagine. He wants to help, but He won't go where He's not invited!

I find that getting to know Him is not difficult. He is only a prayer away.

It starts by simply inviting Him into your life, by accepting Jesus as Lord and savior.

"Jesus, I give my life to you. I believe you died for my sins and was raised from the dead, triumphing over death. I accept you as my

Lord and savior," is all you need to say. Once you have accepted Jesus as Savior, it doesn't mean you will never see trouble; it means He will never leave you alone, and you can call on Him and trust Him. As the psalmist says:

> The LORD is my shepherd;
> I shall not want.
> He makes me to lie down in green pastures;
> He leads me beside the still waters.
> He restores my soul;
> He leads me in the paths of righteousness
> For His name's sake.
> Yea, though I walk through the valley of the
>   shadow of death,
> I will fear no evil;
> For You are with me;
> Your rod and Your staff, they comfort me.
>
> You prepare a table before me in the presence of
>   my enemies;
> You anoint my head with oil;
> My cup runs over.
> Surely goodness and mercy shall follow me all the
>   days of my life;
> And I will dwell in the house of the LORD forever.
>   (Psalm 23:1–6, NKJV)

Don't wait until disaster strikes to remember the name: Jesus. He really, really cares for you and your relationship with Him will take you through the toughest storms.

Whatever you're facing, remember, you can make it (I felt God's attention on this) with God by your side.

13

The Call

When my ex-boyfriend Carter returned from Okinawa, Japan, I felt a lot of anxiety about seeing him again. It may have been five years or so since I last saw him; and we both had gone our separate ways, for various reasons. I essentially moved on. Carter had met someone else and was planning to get married, and so he had moved on, too. One day, I got a call from him asking for his leather jacket back. Annoyed by his request, I decided to give him back everything I had that reminded me of him, including a wool sweater. I still had feelings for him, and once I handed over his items, it would be the last thing connecting us.

I got his jacket, which was much too large for me, but greatly warm, and his wool sweater, and an empty box for packing the items. I had mistakenly washed the sweater and threw it in the dryer, and it shrank to the point where it could have fit a five-year-old. I must admit I felt a bit of vindication when I threw the tiny sweater into the box. *Let him try to fit into that.* For I was disappointed that he would ask for any items back in the first place.

I placed the items in the box, closed the lid and placed the box on the porch, and went for a drive, instructing him to pass by and pick it up, giving him plenty of time so our paths were sure not to cross. As I drove away from the house, with the box sitting alone on the porch, I felt it hard to breathe. I knew I'd never see him again, and a flood of emotions swarmed my mind. I wanted to see him, but I didn't want to have to say goodbye, so I felt it was best this way, to be gone when he arrived.

When I returned, the box was gone, and Carter as well. We spoke a few times on the phone after that, but I knew it was over, though I still held onto a bit of hope. Then, one day, I had a dream.

I was in a church, a warm lovely place, maybe one room, and comfortable. I was kneeling in the pew, when God spoke to me. He told me not to approach the book at the front of the church. I looked to see that indeed there was a large book, maybe two to three feet square, on a table at the front of the church. When He said, don't approach, I immediately obeyed. It was in my heart to obey Him and I gladly complied.

Then, I saw that He gave the same instruction to Carter, who also happened to be close by. When Carter heard the instructions from God to stay away from the book, he disobeyed, and went directly for the book. Suddenly, Carter was outside the church, having been put out by God. Then, I woke.

God seldom speaks to me in dreams. That may have been one of three occasions in my life to date. So I paid attention.

Today, as I thought over the dream and the instruction I got from God to not approach the book, it occurred to me that it was a type of "Garden of Eden test." What if God applies that test to all people, not just to Adam and Eve? So for example, there will be one point in life when we are faced with a decision that seems somewhat insignificant but our obedience or disobedience to God's instructions could be life changing (I felt the Holy Spirit's attention on this).

So when God told Eve not to eat from the tree of the knowledge of good and evil (see Genesis 2:17), maybe Eve wondered, "What's the big deal with the tree?" But it wasn't about the tree. It was about can God trust you? What is in your heart? In a pinch, will you obey His word or do your own thing?

Remember how God tested Abraham in the book of Genesis by telling him to offer his son, Isaac, as a sacrifice? God stopped Abraham before he sacrificed Isaac, but it proved what was in Abraham's heart, that he would withhold nothing from God. (See Genesis 22:1–19.)

So it seems there may be times when God "proves" our hearts, and it's important to listen and follow His instructions, even in the little things. (I feel God's attention on this.)

I struggled with whether to include the dream in this chapter, in case Carter (not his actual name) reads it. How would he respond? Would he see it as the overactive imagination of a woman long gone from his life? Or would he see it as one last caring act, perhaps an invitation to reach for God.

I don't know.

14

Malachi

The only thing Jack ever wanted was to see his son, Peelee, grow up, become a man, and get out of the Bronx. There was Jack sprawled out on the couch imagining his son living uptown, away from all this—the cockroaches scampering across the kitchen sink, the gunshots that echo in every brownstone on the block on weekend nights.

Peelee was all he had. Peelee was going to take his legacy up and out of that place and start over somewhere in the burbs. Then one day, all his dreams crashed!

It happened at the intersection in front of the Billy Goat Restaurant. Jack wasn't paying attention and accidentally knocked Peelee into traffic. And it was the weird way he saw the truck bearing down on Peelee. And Jack couldn't move fast enough to save him. Then time stopped. Jack closed his eyes to block out the sight of blood flowing from under the truck, and when he opened his eyes, he's strapped to a chair in a state hospital.

Dr. Williams is the quirky Hispanic resident who gets the toughest case of her new career. She has to meet Jack in that dark place in his mind and help him find his way back after a nervous breakdown. She has little to go on—Jack is from the Bronx and is believed to have a son.

In each session, she hits on a sore spot. "You have a son, Jack?" she asks while flipping through his chart. That's all it takes, and Jack is having another delusionary episode—we see him struggling to focus on images unfolding on the wall in front of him. Jack tries to tell the story of his pain through those images on the wall. "What do you see, Jack?" she asks.

He sees Jerusalem and Jesus going to the cross, and Mary, His mother, coming to pieces, sobbing and clinging to His arm. "He felt helpless," Jack says, as he tries to explain what he's looking at.

If Jesus could stop everything to save Mary the pain, He would have. "But He can't," Jack says. And we understand that Jack is trying to tell his own painful story, how he wasn't able to save his son, but it's too difficult for him to face head on, so in each session, he speaks through the pain of Jesus.

* * * * * * *

That is a partial summary of my screenplay, *Malachi*, about a dad who lost his son in a horrific car accident and has a mental breakdown. Dr. Williams is the psychiatric resident who steps in to help him.

I labored with that screenplay for several years and finally decided to enter it into an international screenwriting competition for women writers. The prize would be a trip to New York to meet with leaders in the movie industry.

Who would love Jack and Dr. Williams, those broken characters thrown on a page in script format? Apparently, someone did, and *Malachi* earned a 95 percent weighted average in the competition. That meant whoever read the script must have felt the story was worth telling.

But that score was just the first step in the selection process. I still needed to be one of the dozen or so women chosen from hundreds of other applicants to travel to the workshop in New York, where industry professionals would help develop the script.

For the first time in my screenplay writing life I felt as if I might have a shot at getting *Malachi* into the hands of someone who could sail it.

I wanted to believe it; I wanted to believe that I was about to have a breakthrough in my writing career, but as I sat staring at the score on the computer screen, I started to talk myself down. There are hundreds, if not thousands, of other applicants, I told myself, some seasoned industry professionals, so don't get too excited about this score. So I kept it a secret from my friends and family to avoid us all being disappointed. After all, what were the odds of me, some kid from a poor farm in Jamaica, winning a spot in the prestigious competition?

Nevertheless, to increase my odds, I went to God! I knew He could help me, so I took it to Him in prayer. I'd bring up *Malachi* and the competition and say, if there is any way, if it pleases you, if there might be a miracle that could get me on that final list of women chosen to go to New York for the workshop, then please Lord!

The reject letter came some months later. It took me a few minutes to accept the fact that *Malachi* didn't make it to the finals. What could I have done differently? I really felt God's fingerprint was on that script, so what happened? Finally, to console myself, I thought, *I can't rely on people to validate a "work of the Spirit."* At that very moment, I felt the presence of God, as if He was agreeing with me that relying on people to validate the work birthed in this writing ministry might not be the best way to move forward.

* * * * * * *

Near the end of the story, Dr. Williams helps Jack to return to that street corner in the Bronx where his son Peelee was killed by the speeding truck. There was Jack, standing in the middle of the road at 2:00 a.m. holding a small wooden cross covered in plastic flowers, looking at the spot where he last saw Peelee's mutilated body. He lays the cross on the spot, once soaked with Peelee's blood, then he stands slowly, turning in circles, looking at the world through tear-stained glasses. He takes a deep breath and walks away.

Do you have an inspirational story that you'd like to put into script format? Join the conversation and get tips on screenwriting at Faithbridgecafe.com!

15

Rushing Wind

I stared at the message in the draft folder of my phone. "Regret to inform you that I will be leaving at the end of this contract term…" I had been waiting for years to serve God in full time ministry, but did I have the courage to do it—to leave my job, the safety of my apartment and community and move across country to California?

Should I do this? You're calling me to a film and writing ministry Lord? I don't know much about the industry. Where do I begin? The economy is terrible right now? Should I wait?

As I thought about my options, it felt like a "now or never" moment for me. I had the impression that the opportunity of a lifetime would only last as long as the lifetime of the opportunity—like God wouldn't wait forever—as if there were connections to be made and there was a huge time issue.

Finally, I pressed "send." The phone blinked the words "message sent" across the screen. It was done. I gave my job notice that I was leaving. Suddenly, it was as if a cold breeze washed over me. *What did I just do? I could change my mind. I could keep my job. I think they'd be happy to have me stay.* But really, I understood there was no turning back.

I was about to step out in faith, as nerve wrecking and as frightening as it was, I had to go forward! It was as if God was saying: "Have I not commanded you? Be strong and of good courage; do not be afraid, nor be dismayed, for the LORD your God *is* with you wherever you go" (Joshua 1:9).

* * * * * * *

I had no idea how I'd survive the months to come or exactly how one goes about stepping out in full time ministry, but I knew I had to get moving and figure it out.

I had some money saved up and thought I could probably survive on my savings for a few months. It also made sense to have people pray over me before leaving for my journey, to impart some sort of spiritual covering; and I should know more about the basics of evangelism if I'm going to be an evangelist for Christ.

I fought back feelings of total incompetence and reminded myself that many people called to ministry start out this way—with just a vision and a prayer, and a willingness to learn.

Before leaving for California, I tried to prepare myself by getting a better idea of what evangelism involves. I felt called to share the gospel through film and writing, but what does that look like exactly? How do I mentally and spiritually prepare for that step?

I didn't have a lot of money, but I decided to invest a big chunk of it in an evangelism course led by Reinhard Bonnke, the evangelist-firecracker leading many to Christ in Africa. The course would take place in his school in Orlando, Florida, and he would be joined by some other highly respected ministers, including Evangelist Daniel Kolenda and Reverend Teresia Wairimu Kinyanjui.

On a Sunday, I loaded up my two dogs, Maximus and Simba, and headed South for Reverend Bonnke's school of evangelism. As I headed down interstate Highway 85, I felt the exhaustion in my mind from years of pushing papers and working to eat, but not really living. This was my chance to live the life I've always wanted—to impact my world for Christ!

I thought about all the teachers at the School, some flying in from various parts of the world, like Reverend Bonnke and Reverend Kolenda, who would be taking time off from their Africa evangelistic crusades to teach at the school during the four-day session.

I felt small compared to them, and a bit insignificant, but I reminded myself that their greatness rested in God, and that if God could use them, He could use me too, seeing that He is no respecter of persons (see Acts 10:34).

As I drove to Florida, I had one major prayer: "Lord, I pray for an anointing for the ministry and for the days ahead. Please impart strength and power for whatever challenges I will face."

A day later, I arrived at the School tired physically, but my heart was filled with anticipation of how God would move in the coming days. During the sessions, I listened eagerly as the teachers shared their incredible stories, while jotting down notes of how to witness effectively.

The stories themselves were remarkable, telling of miracles in Africa, people getting out of wheelchairs, etc., but the underlying theme was the same: as an evangelist of the gospel, one must fully commit to God, walk in integrity, and be led by the Holy Spirit.

Beyond the practical lessons on evangelism, we had moments of prayer and spiritual impartations. One event in particular would change my life forever!

It happened on a Wednesday afternoon at lunch. As it was the custom after the morning session, some of the teachers joined the students in the lunchroom. On this particular day as I lined up with my classmates at the lunchroom door, I noticed that Rev. Teresia was sitting at one of the tables with her colleagues. I saw that there was an empty seat directly in front of her. My heart started to race. She is one of the women I admire most in the world, not because she is rich or a movie star personality, but because she is courageous and a powerful woman of God. The hand of God is strong on her life.

I wanted to sit and have a talk with her about serving God, but I was already nervous at the prospect of trying to have a conversation with someone of her prominence. A tall woman with a strong presence, she carries herself with confidence and her words are striking. I'm soft spoken and sometimes shy. In my mind, I could already see myself blundering.

Nevertheless, I knew it was a once in a lifetime opportunity that might never come again, so before getting my lunch I left the long line and hurried over to her table. "May I sit here?" I asked, with a timid smile. "Someone is sitting there," she said. I was about to turn and crawl to another table when she added, "You can sit on that chair." It was the chair right beside the one I had wanted. I nodded eagerly and dropped my pocketbook on the chair and went to get my lunch plate.

As amazing as Rev. Teresia is, I wasn't reaching for her; I was reaching for the power of God I sensed on her life. I wanted His cutting edge and bold presence to occupy my life the same way it does hers! I wanted a connection with God on that same level—whatever it is that propels her to walk with such confidence into a room and speak with such ease about her God—that very thing, I wanted! I wanted more of the Holy Spirit!

When I returned with my lunch, I saw that she was flanked on both sides by people eager to speak to her. I felt sorry for her because she was hardly allowed a moment to eat her lunch in peace. I'm sorry to say that despite my pity, I didn't behave any better than the rest of the crowd. I politely interrupted her conversation and told her I'd like to speak to her at some point during the lunch. She brought order by telling each of us which one would speak first, etc. The short African man in the suit had an appointment, he would go first. I was third. I was satisfied with that.

I sat quietly and waited for the first two people to finish and then I formerly introduced myself and told her of my interest in serving God in film. "Women prepared Jesus for His departure," I told her, "and I believe we will be instrumental in preparing the way for His return." She listened attentively, nodding occasionally.

In her quiet power and humility, she shared that she had a similar interest. She then shared some of her plans, remarking that by the grace of God, enormous doors are opening to her ministry in Africa.

Before leaving, I asked her to pray for me and this ministry I felt God has called me to.

Sitting across from her, I could see why she is affectionately referred to as "Mom" by the many who meet her. Behind her stern demeanor is a warm, Godly, maternal spirit.

I wanted her to pray for me because I admired the work God is doing in her life—He has built a strong, mature ministry. I had a little fledgling ministry, but what I saw in her gave me hope.

She reached across the lunch table and took my hand and we bowed our heads and she prayed. At the end of the prayer, I thanked her and headed back to the seminar room for the second part of the evangelism session. But as I was walking something amazing happened!

I had an open vision of anointing oil on my forehead in the shape of a cross. I felt the fresh oil on my forehead, but it was in the spirit, not visible. I had a revelation that I had received an anointing for the ministry and the days ahead. It was a powerful spiritual impartation. The implications of this anointing, blessing, and impartation would become apparent in time.

I am learning to expect fabulous things from God—to go to Him with a bold desire to serve Him in the strongest and most committed way possible. Thank God, I don't have to be perfect or glamorous, just courageous and fully committed. I just need to be bold enough to take a step of faith!

This doesn't guarantee an easy road, but I've learned that the prayers and blessings of others will help sustain me when the road is difficult, providing a special covering as I move forward with God.

God is willing to bless and equip those who trust in Him, and He's able to do far above what we can ask or think (see Ephesians 3:20). For those who trust in and rely on God, then God Himself will be their rear guard (see Isaiah 58:8).

* * * * * * *

After Jesus received the Holy Spirit, right before He started His ministry, He was taken immediately into the desert to be tested and tried (see Matthew 4:1).

That seems to be the pattern for those who want to serve God. In my case, my "testing" would take place in the dry, dusty Mojave Desert in California.

For I am the Lord your God who takes hold of your right hand and say to you, "Do not fear; I will help you." (Isaiah 41:13, NIV)

16

The Migration

Author's Note: One of the biggest problems people face when they step out in faith is poor planning (I feel the Holy Spirit's attention on this). I didn't have much of a plan when I started full time ministry and winged it, often creating a lot of unnecessary stress for myself, as the following story will show.

But at least I stepped out (I felt the Holy Spirit's attention on this as well)!

* * * * * * *

After my evangelism training, I packed up my minivan (including my two pups) and headed for California, convinced that God had called me to launch out and begin a ministry in writing and film.

I had no idea what to expect as I drove through miles and miles of lonely desert highway. The journey would try my faith, bending it to a breaking point, but I found that the more I stayed the course the more I found God flowing in on the hot desert breeze.

The journey took approximately six days and is more or less summarized here.

Day 1. I treasure the quiet time on the road with the Lord and spend very little time on the phone talking to friends or family. I want this time to reflect on what it will mean to step out in faith in full time ministry. Will I see my screenplay produced? I can't explain the exhilaration I feel, with just me and God on this journey together and the open road.

I only need to get to California. I have just enough money to cover the drive there and take care of about a month's worth of expenses. I have no family, no friends or contacts in the area, but I plan on trusting God to make the necessary connections happen.

Day 2. I'm driving through Georgia and the Carolinas, my soul taking deep breaths as I watch miles and miles of farmland and marshes unfold before me.

Sometimes, I get a special surprise when I go around the bend in a road and spot an old historic bridge, or glimpse streams of fresh running water. I feel quiet inside and avoid phone calls, but sometimes listen to music—some Mozart, some gospel. I have lots of time to think about my screenplays. I pray, and I try to hear from God.

Day 3. The greenery of South-Central US is starting to disappear, and the desert land of Texas is beginning to fill my view. I often drive for miles along Route 10, mostly dry dusty road, before seeing another soul.

My fate is truly in the hands of God. My car can't break down, have a flat tire, or run out of gas; not out here, not in the middle of nowhere. The road seems to go on forever. I'm trying to get to a small town before dark to find a hotel.

I try not to focus on the loneliness of the road, and it seems to me that I feel the very real presence of God. *I need you God to take care of me now.* At sunset, the light is lovely here. Orange and yellow hues filter across the rocky hills and sprawl over the highway, bringing lovely flickering colors that make the desert seem to dance.

Day 4. I have driven hundreds of miles in four days and I'm somewhere in New Mexico.

I feel achy all over, and I can feel the romance and intrigue about this new adventure begin to slip away from me and morph into a strong sense of fatigue and exhaustion. The trip is more expensive than I had hoped, and it troubles me that I no longer have enough money to stay at a decent hotel—not if I want to have enough to pay for the apartment in California.

The one thing I need in all this is good sleep each night, and I dread the thought of a "flea motel." I will have to make some adjustments to my plans, at least where lodging is concerned, but not tonight. I pay the nearly hundred dollars for a good hotel.

Day 5. I'm somewhere near the California border; I think maybe I'm in Arizona.

I'm at a "flea motel" and just registered for the night. I reasoned that I could put up with a lousy bed and that it was more important to save enough for the apartment and expenses once I arrive in California. The "lobby" of the motel is a tiny cubicle filled with the smell of incense and cheap air freshener. I paid less than $40 and have a key to a room near the lobby. Before unloading my luggage, I go to the room to look around.

As I open the door, a warm stench blows past me. The carpet is sticky from the afternoon dew, and there's a large dead cockroach on the bathroom floor. The curtains hold a mousy brown color, and the towels have a vague yellow tint. I walk around the room for a moment and pray. *I'm not sure I can handle this.*

As I walk back to the front of the building, I can see my tired pups looking out the car window, eyes wide and tails wagging. I must make a decision. I can't afford the fancy hotel next door and I'm exhausted. The flea motel is the best I can do. It's late at night and I need to get some rest. I don't want to go back on that highway.

I notice all the large trucking rigs parked along the outer rim of the parking lot. I remember the smell in the room and the dirty rugs. I stop pacing and go back inside the motel office and hand in the key. I won't be staying here.

I sit in my car for a minute wondering if I made the right decision—I know what the second option is, and I don't like the idea at all. I drive to the fancy hotel next door and park near the entrance, pull a blanket from the back seat, and scoot my legs onto the passenger seat.

My pups snuggle in next to me and quickly fall off to sleep. I wish for a moment that I could be as worry free and relaxed as they are.

I check my rearview and side mirrors to make sure I have a clear view of all my van doors and that there aren't any large shrubs next to the vehicle where someone can hide. I want to be able to spot anyone approaching.

Then, I try to settle in for the night. As I lay there in the front seat and look up at the hotel windows circling my minivan—tired travelers who were lucky enough to have a hot bath and a nice, clean hotel room—I begin to question my common sense. I wonder if I hadn't just made a dumb move by packing up my van and making the drive across country. I try to ignore the windows circling my vehicle, but as I close my eyes, it feels very much like trying to sleep under a glass jar.

Around three hours later, I wake to the sounds of people chatting as they walk by my van. My head is in a fog but I'm grateful that I got a little rest. I try to remember which State I'm in, and which highway I have been traveling. I shake off the sleep and try to find a Starbucks.

Day 6. My mind is on autopilot. I never knew I could feel so tired and restless. *Was this a mistake, Lord?* All I hear is silence, except for the wind blowing outside my car window. *Was this a mistake? I could cut my losses and drive back to New England. How will I survive in California? I don't have family there…God, what should I do?*

The road seems to go on forever. Several hours into day six of driving, I pull into a hotel parking lot and park the car near the entrance. I reach for the blanket in the backseat and lay across the front seats. My pups cuddle in next to me. It's an instant replay of last night. I try to shut the image out of my mind—me, in plain view, sleeping in the front seat of my car.

My mind rambles back to the day I graduated from law school—my family sitting in the audience beaming with pride—if they could see me now. I never imagined that this would be my lot. Did I hear God correctly? Is God in this road trip of mine, or am I a victim of my own imagination? *But I'm sure God has called me to do this!* I spend several minutes trying to convince myself before falling off to sleep.

Day 7. I'm so tired I can barely think straight. I haven't had a good night sleep in about three days. It might have been the ninth hour into my journey on day seven, my eyes nearly dazed over, my body aching from days of driving, when I glance over to my right and see a sign that reads, "Welcome to California." A tear wells up inside me as I take a tired breath and whisper, "I'm here, Lord."

Stepping out in faith and driving across country to California was one of the toughest things I have ever done. I left behind all that was familiar, and all that I had counted on for peace and safety, like family and the ocean, my church and friends.

I'd love to say I was always 100 percent sure I was making the right decision, but I was simply more sure than not.

In the days ahead, the journey would put an enormous amount of pressure on my faith and mind and reveal my weaknesses and strengths. Mostly, it would launch me into position to totally rely on God.

When I left New England for the cross-country drive, I never intended to sleep in my car, and it's not something I'd ever recommend. I took a huge risk. By the grace of God, I was not harmed.

During my time with God on the road and in California, my faith would tumble along until finally, I would learn to trust Him, so that today as I sit here typing this, I can say I know God as an incredible friend and King.

The California desert with its lonely roads and harsh climate would serve as an incubator for our relationship and would prove to be a most worthwhile journey! But it would not be an easy one, as the following stories will show.

17

Mojave Desert

"God is in control" was all she said in her message. Shortly after arriving to the Mojave Desert in California, the stranger's text message appeared in my inbox. Apparently, she had meant to send the message to her niece but didn't realize that I was the new occupant of her niece's old phone number. Before that moment, I had never heard from the stranger, but I would soon learn that the words that found its way to my phone's inbox had an assignment. It would undergird me as I entered one of the toughest storms of my life!

* * * * * * *

After moving across country to California, I was unable to afford living in Los Angeles, so I settled for a dusty little apartment in the Mojave Desert—the last place in the world I wanted to be—but it was an easy commute to LA, and it was cheap.

I managed to keep a good amount of optimism while I settled into a desert lifestyle, but one day, I found myself in a perfect storm—a combination of two forces colliding—illness *and* isolation. I was alone on the other side of the Country, away from the support and care of friends and family, when I became very sick. I had never had those two storms collide before, illness and isolation, and it became an incredible source of anxiety for me.

It started with flu symptoms, extreme tiredness and dizziness, then difficulty breathing. Whatever illness had me bound up drained me of physical strength. I could hardly drive my car or focus.

I had trouble standing and walking. I felt sick to my stomach, woozy, and I had trouble taking a deep breath. The overall sense of weakness was overwhelming.

I had been battling an infected tooth and thought that was the problem, that somehow, I had become "toxic." But after dental treatment, I only felt worse.

As the sickness lingered, I lost all desire to pray. All I could think about was how lousy I felt, and how deeply alone. As I meditated on that fact, I felt trapped, and frustrated with myself for having moved to California. I thought about the job I gave up and the community I left behind. I felt as if I was messing up my life.

One evening, about three days after the worst symptoms began, I managed to get myself to the emergency room. The visiting physician, without giving me a physical exam and after just listening to the symptoms, said I had a case of the flu and sent me home; but this felt unlike anything I had ever experienced. This was not *just* the flu.

One afternoon, when nothing else seemed to be working, in desperation, I went in search of a prayer partner. In truth, I just didn't want to be alone and I wanted someone else to remind God that I was in trouble.

I had been attending a church about ten miles away, so I drove there in hopes of finding the pastor, or anyone willing to pray with me, but the church was closed. I then decided to find a church in my neighborhood and found one about five minutes away. *If only I could find someone to sit with me and pray!*

As I turned into the church parking lot, I saw a middle-aged woman with short, dirty blonde hair standing at the church door with a key in her hand, locking the door. Then, she turned and headed towards her car.

I got out of my car and walked over to her.

"Hi, do you have a minute? Sorry to inconvenience you…" When she turned to look at me, I saw that she was a bit irritated.

"What is it?" she asked, impatiently.

"I don't feel well. I'm not from here, and don't know who to turn to. I wonder if there is someone here who can pray with me."

"Well," she quipped, "I'm on my way to work and I'm running late. There is no one inside. There are benches behind the church. You can go sit there until you feel better." With that, she got in her car and drove off.

I stood alone in the parking lot in front of the locked church door and tried to catch my breath. I felt like crying but didn't. After a few seconds, I got in my car and drove back to my apartment.

Inside my desert apartment, I didn't feel like praying, but mumbled something about "no weapon formed against me can prosper and by His stripes I am healed." I paced about and tried to remember other scriptures I had "stored up" for times like this. "The Lord is my Shepherd…I can do all things through Christ…"

Finally, I went to bed and tried to ignore the symptoms, especially the tightness in my chest and the short breaths. By the mercy of God, I fell off to sleep for about five hours.

For the next few days, my symptoms didn't improve, so I tossed around an exit plan in my mind. I reasoned that this—the desert heat, the harsh sandy air, California, the illness, the pressure—was too much for me. I missed the ocean and hated the harsh desert landscape. I missed my family and friends. I told myself that the moment I had the strength, I would head home. *Mom was right. This move to California was a bad idea.*

It was around this time that I sat down on my bed and flipped through the text messages in the inbox of my phone, trying to determine who to reach out to, when I came across the message that was sent to me several months earlier, from the stranger. She (or he) had sent it to me by mistake, but I wanted to believe that it wasn't accidental. "God is in control," the message said. I began to type a message to the stranger.

"Please pray for me," I wrote.

"Who are you and what's going on?" Looking at the response, I felt a tear well up inside me, roll down my cheek and fall onto my lap.

"I'm the one you wrote to accidentally a few months ago. I quit my job and moved to California to serve the Lord in full time ministry, and I'm having a difficult time. I don't want to tell my family or friends back home because I don't want them to worry. I'd appreciate it if you'd pray."

I had never done anything like that before, send a text message SOS to a total stranger; but I feared that if I had reached out to my family and friends, the panic I felt brewing inside would take off and I'd be in a real fix. The stranger helped me to stay calmer—to limit my emotional response.

The stranger told me that there was a minister in San Diego I could contact if I'd like to, and told me to stay in touch and let him/her know if I needed anything. I sent back a text message asking for prayer for my health and finances. The stranger wrote back:

> Just believe that by GOD'S stripes you are healed. Most gracious FATHER, I stand in your mist and (we) are asking, believing and also receiving that her body is healed from all ailments, her mind is clear without cloudiness, her heart is filled and not hurting or broken, we claim an overflow of abundance.
>
> FATHER GOD, I ask that you feed Del until she want no more. LORD we love you, we cherish you and we magnify your Holy Name. Lord, you said in your word that you are our light and salvation whom shall we fear, you are the strength of our lives of who shall we be afraid, even when our enemies and our foes encamped around us they stumbled and fell. AMEN.

I read the prayer and wept.

The following evening, I was still battling feelings of isolation, anxiety and intense flu-like symptoms. I knew in my head that God is stronger than my problems; that He is "in control," as the stranger suggested, but I had trouble connecting with that reality. I had trouble trusting Him. In my heart, I wanted to walk in faith and be strong, but felt stuck in my fears.

I tried to reason with myself. *You've got to pull up. You can't crash like this!* I was congested to the point where I felt faint. I knew some of it was caused by anxiety, but I couldn't break loose from it.

I paced around my apartment looking at the inspirational words I had pasted on the walls. One message on a calendar said, "Be still and know that I am God." I wanted to be still; I wanted to be obedient, but I couldn't seem to pull my mind around.

Outside my apartment door, people were walking along with friends, mothers were playing with their children, and others gathered on their porch for a barbecue—all strangers oblivious to my struggle.

What happens if I really get sick? I mean, is it just the flu? I can't breathe. What if it's pneumonia? I checked my shallow breathing, the heaviness in my throat and chest, the headache, the woozy feeling inside. I felt faint. *It's probably pneumonia.*

As I paced the floor of my apartment, the space seemed small and hot and confusing. Frustrated, I went to my car and got some empty boxes. *I'm going to pack and get out of here! I can't live this way. I refuse to live this way!* Back inside my apartment, I didn't have the strength to pack the boxes. *I'll wait until morning.*

I took a hot bath, hoping to free up my breathing and relax my mind. I could see the promises of God I had pasted on the wall. One promise was just the word, "Deliverance." *Where is the deliverance, Lord?* I was angry now and irritable, exhausted from not sleeping well. *I don't want the desert experience—I hate the desert! Why did I move to this place? Did God call me here? Really Lord, what is this?*

"Don't be afraid. I'm here," I felt Him say. I tried to pull my mind around and calm my fears, but it was useless.

The summer days had been hot, long and dusty in the Desert, but somehow, I had found God in the barrenness. I spoke to Him and relied on Him more in the Desert than anywhere else I had ever been. But when the challenges escalated, when I got sick and felt weak and helpless, my faith took a hit! I felt stuck in a perfect storm! I felt bowed over in fear.

The nighttime was the most difficult! I knew, as I laid there trying to catch my breath and relax my mind, that I needed to continue to trust Him, to remember that He is with me, and to not panic. But I felt gridlocked by the symptoms, and troubled by the constant thought: "You have nobody here and you are really sick. You are alone, and you have no one. Who will help you?"

I had been sick in a foreign place before. When I was a missionary in Japan, there were days when I didn't feel well, but this was different. In Japan, I had other missionaries to turn to, and the illness was nothing like this. In Mojave, not only was I alone, but the symptoms were strange and intense! At times, I thought I might drop to the floor. I had to lean against something to avoid collapsing; something was obviously wrong.

If it was a type of flu, I wasn't familiar, and it was taking my immune system on a spin. About a week into the illness, feeling achy, woozy, and beat up, I eased myself out of bed and went into prayer. I prayed for healing, and kept confessing, "By His stripes I am healed." I didn't feel that way. My head felt congested, and my breathing was shallow. I felt as if I was suffocating.

Finally, I got dressed and picked up my pocketbook, and slowly headed out the door. *I'll go to the emergency room. At least there, I won't be alone.*

"Relax," I felt God say. "When you hear, do as I say!" In my heart, I knew He was telling me, urging me: "I am here and will help you! You need to calm down and trust Me!" *How can I calm down when I feel like this?* The idea seemed irrational.

As I walked to my car, I was taking short, rapid breaths and feeling woozy. I felt like falling into His arms and sobbing.

Driving down the street, I stared at all the signs lining the road, hoping to see one that read "H" or "Hospital." I stopped at a red light at the corner of Twentieth Street West and decided to turn on the radio to get my mind off the symptoms. I found a Christian radio station. A man was reading a scripture. He sounded Roman Catholic. I was about to meet up with my deliverance!

"God is our refuge and strength," he said. Suddenly, in the time it took for the light to change from red to green, I felt a shift! It was as if everything went into slow motion and the words the man had just spoken, "God is our refuge and strength," connected with my heart and triggered my faith!

The words streaming from the radio, each one like drops of water in a glass, were *connecting* and filling my heart with faith!

> God is our refuge and strength,
> A very present help in trouble.
> Therefore we will not fear,
> Even though the earth be removed,
> And though the mountains be carried into the
>   midst of the sea;
> *Though* its waters roar *and* be troubled,
> *Though* the mountains shake with its swelling. *Selah*
>
> There is a river whose streams shall make glad the
>   city of God,
> The holy place of the tabernacle of the Most High.
> God *is* in the midst of her, she shall not be moved;
> God shall help her, just at the break of dawn.
> The nations raged, the kingdoms were moved;
> He uttered His voice, the earth melted.
> The Lord of hosts is with us;
> The God of Jacob is our refuge. *Selah*
>
> Come, behold the works of the Lord,
> Who has made desolations in the earth.
> He makes wars cease to the end of the earth;
> He breaks the bow and cuts the spear in two;
> He burns the chariot in the fire.
> Be still and know that I am God;
> I will be exalted among the nations,
> I will be exalted in the earth!
> The Lord of hosts *is* with us; The God of Jacob
>   is our refuge. *Selah.* (Psalm 46:1–11, NKJV)

As I listened to His words, peace washed over me and my anxiety lifted! I relaxed my shoulders and my breathing. For the first time in several days, I took a deep breath. I went from panic to peace in about two minutes. It was as if the scripture cut away the burr from my emotions. I had never seen words go to work like that before. As I listened to the words, faith arose, and the fear fell off me like dry leaves from a tree.

In other words, the word of God reached into my soul and ignited faith like fire on dry grass. It had something to do with the timing of the message, but I felt too, the very real love of God effectively releasing me from my fears. It was as if He reached down from Heaven and rescued me! Suddenly, I had a surge of energy!

> For the word of God is alive and active [I felt the Holy Spirit's attention on that]. Sharper than any double-edged sword. It penetrates even to dividing soul and spirit, joints and marrow; it judges the thoughts and attitudes of the heart. (Hebrews 4:12, NIV)

And God says, "So shall My word be that goes forth from My mouth; it will not return to Me void, but it shall accomplish what I please, and it shall prosper *in the thing* for which I sent it" (Isaiah 55:11, NKJV).

Halleluiah!

In retrospect, I see that the issue that confronted me during that moment when I was sick in Mojave was not the sickness and sense of isolation—that was a very real problem—but the bigger issue was fear. I allowed fear to dominate my thinking instead of the promises of God, and the fact of His presence and protection! In my weakness, I lost heart; but by the grace of God, I would regain my faith and courage through the amazing active power of His word!

Those same mega flu symptoms would return a few more times while I lived in the desert but would never again get such a hold over me! The promise of God to be "a very present help in trouble" stayed fresh in my mind.

The storm taught me a bit about how God works. He is incredibly protective of those who step out on His word. I appreciate too that if I had the usual go-to, that I may never have experienced the "power of His words" in that storm. When it was just me and God in a desert place filled with strangers, I (eventually) learned to connect with His heart and to lean on Him. I learned from Him that He can be trusted, and that He is able and willing to deliver me from harm; that in times of trouble, He is not far off.

When I needed Him most, He showed up! He didn't bring scolding in His wings. I never sensed anger or disapproval emanating from Him, only an outstretched hand. He didn't reprimand me for being slow to believe and trust. He merely did what He does best— He ran a rescue and brought reassurance!

It meant everything to me that He reached over the airways and connected with my soul that day in the car. Yes, He used a pastor to deliver the message, but I am certain that the words, the sentiment, and the love were from Him.

The breakthrough experience gave meaning to our time together in the desert. His efforts were effective—I was being taught to trust Him and receive His word, to lean on Him in times of trouble; and I was seeing with my own eyes, experiencing in my own heart, the power of His words, the power of His presence, and the level of His love for me!

The answer is to trust Him and to calm down even when it seems the earth be removed from under one's feet, to actively remember that He is near! He is present in the "storm" and says, "Take courage." (See Joshua 1:9.)

As Jesus reasssured His desciples: "In this world you will have trouble. But take heart! I have overcome the world" (John 16:33, NIV).

In case I forgot to say it before, thank You, God! Thank You for never failing me nor forsaking me! In Jesus's name, amen.

18

Stormy Flight

I t was a winter day after work when I felt prompted to visit a church in downtown Hollywood. Devon Franklin, a former executive of Sony Pictures, was the guest speaker. As he took the microphone, I could tell by the very first words he spoke that the message was for me. "God has called you here tonight because He wants you to understand what worry is…worry gives your mind away to troubles… God says, 'I want you to master that thing!'"[11]

The congregation was riveted by his words, and a string of "amens" rang out as he spoke. Many in the audience, like me, left everything behind in their hometown and travelled to Hollywood to invest in the dream they felt God had for them. Some brought a one-way bus ticket and others, like me, drove across country.

We had other things in common as well—we were all tired from the journey and thirsty for any word of encouragement, and we all struggled with worry.

It was weighing on us, the scope of what we were trying to accomplish—whether it was to write the faith-based screenplay, make the feature film, or land a respectable role in a decent movie—it felt nearly impossible. It was easy to worry, stepping out on "water" as we did; the water in this case being the word of God and a prayer.

As Mr. Franklin spoke, judging from the strong "amens" and seeing how intensely everyone listened, I could tell that worry had been our nemesis—that one thing we all struggled with. I listened intently as he continued. "Matthew 6 says, 'Do not worry about tomorrow...' I'm here to tell you, anything you worried about a solution for, God has a solution!"[12]

And we needed His solutions—how do we pay our bills while trying to launch a new career—acting on weekends for some or writing a screenplay long into the evening for others. Most of us were stepping into an arena that was totally new to us, and often worried about failing.

The congregation of around a thousand people were all intensely watching the animated and dynamic Franklin and gawking at all that he has accomplished when he reminded us that he is just as we are, facing worry and working to overcome it.

> I'm not preaching something I don't know...
> Man, you want to talk about going through
> something—start your own company. Step out
> on faith! Leave a very, very, very, very nice job.
> You want to talk about some faith. You want to
> talk about worrying about tomorrow? And God
> has been challenging me...To deal with worry,
> anything you've been anxious about doing, or
> fearful of doing... Do it![13]

To the hundreds of hungry souls chasing a dream in Hollywood, to see a man like Devon Franklin who stepped out in faith, who understood what it meant to risk everything, really meant a lot to us. He left his comfy job at Sony to start his own faith-based film production company. He understood what we faced as trailblazers, as hopefuls. He pushed us to follow after God, to do hard things, and to trust the results to God without worrying.

Mr. Franklin explained that worry is designed to take your attention off what God is doing in your life in the present moment. Then he challenged us by asking, "If you believe God on the level you say you do, what would you do now that you've been afraid to do all year? Do you really believe God is in your corner? Do you really believe He has it all under control?" [14]

He closed his message with a simple but powerful prayer.

> Dear heavenly Father… change the worrier heart and replace it with the warrior heart…the spirit of the warrior is determined to fight not with their strength, but with Your strength…I come against anxiety, I come against fear, I come against complacency, I come against timidity…I cast down worry, in the name of Jesus…! [15]

One day during my walk of faith, when I *wasn't* doing a very good job of walking in faith, but was fearful and worried, in my heart, I felt God say, "Our love is stronger than your emotions!"

He was saying in effect that our relationship, our love-based covenant, our Jesus-based relationship is stronger than my feelings of inadequacy and fear! He was reminding me that we have something unshakable! The bond between us flows into the supernatural realm, and throughout eternity. He was saying that what we have between us is so strong, I need not worry.

He hadn't given up on me because I stumbled about. Throughout it all, He only had that one admonition: "Don't worry!" In other words, "Be courageous!"

* * * * * * *

If you've stepped out in faith and find yourself in a challenging position—maybe you're homeless, or it's a lot more difficult than you anticipated—instead of worrying, the best solution is always to take it to God, to trust Him. Talk to Him and lean on Him. He won't let you down! He wants to help you! His heart is for you, not against you. (See Romans 8:31.)

He wants to lift you up and encourage you. (See Philippians 4:19.) Maybe that's the very reason you're reading this now. God wants to show Himself strong on your behalf! Don't give up. You have greatness in you, and God will help you (I feel the Holy Spirit's attention on that).

> For the eyes of the Lord run to and fro throughout the whole earth, to show Himself strong on behalf of those whose heart is loyal to Him… (2 Chronicles 16:9, NKJV)

By dying for you on the cross, Jesus purchased the amazing opportunity that allows you to approach the throne room of God and ask for help; and those who ask for help will not be turned away. (See John 6:37.)

19

The Navigator

I used to work at an airport and saw how the ground crew used a "pushback" tractor to get the airplane away from the gate. (The plane needs to be at a safe distance from the gate before firing up the engines to avoid damage to the building from engine blast.) The pushback tractor has a rig that is fastened to the front wheels of the plane that is used to gently push the plane back.

Right before takeoff, the pilot surrenders control of the plane to the pushback driver. Then the pushback driver attaches a "bypass pin," which means steering the plane switches from the cockpit to the pushback tractor. The pushback steers the plane to a safe distance away from the building, then returns control to the cockpit.

Once, while sitting in one of those planes that was being pushed back, I could tell that the captain had surrendered the power to move the vehicle to the guy driving the pushback tractor because the plane engines were quiet. Once the plane cleared the gate, the pushback disconnected from the plane and the plane engines kicked in as the pilot began to line up with the runway for takeoff. It involved a lot of communication, precision, and coordination. It took the pilot being willing to relinquish control to the pushback driver because he had no other way of safely reversing the plane. It took trust. What's my point?

When we encounter obstacles in life, it helps to remember that we are part of a greater team (I felt the Holy Spirit's attention on that). It is a coordinated effort. We have the Holy Spirit who gives us wisdom and shows us things to come (Isaiah 11:2); we have angels that are dispatched to protect us (Psalm 91:11); and we have God who loves us and gives us access to His Kingdom (John 3:16). We have Jesus who died for our sins and intercedes for us at the right hand of the Father (see Romans 8:34).

This is what I'm learning on this journey: the born-again believer is part of an incredibly powerful team! When we realize that there is an entire crew working to help us in life, we are less inclined to worry. But the "crew" can only be effective to the extent that we communicate (pray), follow instructions, trust, and at times, surrender control.

So instead of worrying, "have faith in God" (Mark 11:22, NIV).

> Now faith is being sure of what we hope for and certain of what we do not see. (Hebrews 11:1, NIV)

* * * * * *

If you'd like to accept Jesus as Lord, or if you've gotten off trail and would like to return to God, now is your chance. No matter how many times you've messed up and no matter how outrageous the sin, go to Him! He is the master of recovery and restoration, and He will make it a point to help you! Give Him a chance to show you how much He cares about your life. Whether it's fear or worry or something else, He is willing and able to help you!

If you're not sure what to say, try simply saying: "I believe God raised Jesus from the dead, and I confess with my mouth that Jesus is Lord. Come into my heart Lord Jesus; please forgive me for my sins and lead me forward. I trust my life to your Hands." (I felt the Holy Spirit's attention on that last sentence!)

* * * * * *

The remaining stories will show, like the others in this book, that the faith walk is a process. (There are some days when we all need to be reminded not to worry.) More importantly, it shows how God stays the course and will always be there when you need Him!

A Trailblazer's Journey to:

PARIS, FRANCE

20

The Vision Board

I have a flight shortly and I have no idea how this trip will affect my life. I feel fearless and frightened at the same time, as if I am about to get into my own personal two-engine Cessna airplane and take flight, solo, into the clouds. I'm taking my little savings and pouring it into a dream, that dream in the photo on my vision board with me sitting at a café in Paris. It is absolutely impractical to do it now, while I am struggling as a writer, while I have so many other things that need my savings and attention.

One day, as I sat in front of my vision board, that two-by-three cardboard that sits on my desk, with pictures and words that represent all my dreams, I realized that none of them have manifested. There, to my right, is the photo of a café in Paris, with a small picture of me superimposed onto it. "I will sit at a café in Paris," I told myself as I taped the photo to my vision board. And then there is that photo of the Wailing Wall in Jerusalem; and on and on, making for a total of eight visions, eight un-manifested dreams.

Later, as I was going about the little town I live in, passing the same stores, the same traffic lights, and pulling into the same gas station, while I was at the gas pump, I paused. I thought about my bank account and how much the trip to Paris would cost. *Should I go? Can I afford to take this trip?* It would be expensive, away from the familiar, and it meant traveling alone to the far side of the world.

As I questioned my decision, wondering if I was wrong to book those flights, my eyes focused on a graveyard in the distance. I thought about the bodies buried in those graves. They all had a chance to live their dreams, to take risks; how many of them followed through? I knew one day I would breathe my last breath. What will be my testimony? What songs will I have sung? What dreams will I have fulfilled? What un-lived dreams will still be posted to my vision board? (I felt the Holy Spirit's attention on that.)

It was then that I decided that yes, I would go. I would spend my savings. I would take the journey. I would take the risks.

As I was getting ready for my trip and searching through papers on my desk, I came across a note, a message that I had received from the Lord on October 20, 2011. It says simply, "I will take care of you." I tucked the note in my passport and took a deep breath.

21

Notre Dame

My second outing in Paris involved a drive to the City Center. I was thankful as I clung to the steering wheel and entered the millionth roundabout, that I had GPS, and even though I was sleep deprived, I was doing miraculously well at merging with traffic and deciphering the signs at the side of the road, most of them in French.

I was laser focused, a bit tense, and staring straight ahead, when suddenly I caught a glimpse of a large structure in my peripheral vision, just off to my right. I turned for a quick glance, and what I saw took my breath away. "Notre Dame!" I said out loud, and suddenly, as quickly as the image came into view, it was gone, leaving me fighting back a tear and unraveling a string of emotions.

"Notre Dame!" I said again. The massive structure took me by surprise, and was captivating in a way I can't explain—it is a strong symbol of resilience, not just for Parisians, but for my own soul, and the soul of everyone who have had to rebuild after a tragedy.

I, like millions of others, watched the news when the great architectural wonder took a blaze several months ago, with flames that destroyed large sections of the mammoth structure. Now, here I was driving along the same street where the tragedy took place. But what delight it was to see it recovering, what hope! It was flanked with ballasts and scaffolding on the far-left side, as far as I could see, and it stood majestic and daring and lovely, still. It emitted a certain sprit of resilience, even courage.

Later, after parking my car, I headed back to the structure and stood a while in a flood of other tourists taking snapshots of a special piece of world history. The cathedral has managed to remain charming and imposing, even after a collapsed roof, smoke and water damage. It was one of the special highlights of my trip to Paris.

Notre Dame Cathedral is inspiring because it has a solid stone structure and is hard to fully destroy, reminding us very much of our lives in Christ Jesus. Trouble comes to us all, and sometimes does significant damage, but we have Christ as our foundation; now all we need is the courage to start again.

If you have experienced a major "fire" in your life, whether it's illness, a failed relationship or death of a loved one, don't give up hope. Trust Jesus as your Lord and Savior and watch Him rebuild those broken places.

If you don't know Jesus as Lord, here is a simple prayer from the Billy Graham Association that can totally and wonderfully transform your life.

Prayer of Salvation

"Dear Lord Jesus, I know I am a sinner, and I ask for your forgiveness. I believe you died for my sins and rose from the dead. I trust and follow you as my Lord and Savior. Guide my life and help me to do your will. In your name, amen."[16]

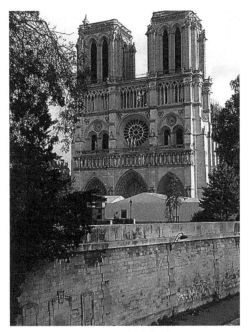

Notre Dame Cathedral, 2019.

The rebuilding of the Notre Dame Cathedral, Paris, 2019.

22

Eiffel Tower

"I've dreamt of this all my life," I said to the stranger as we crossed the street on the Champ de Mars; but I wasn't just speaking to her, I wanted the world to know, and she just happened to be within hearing distance. "Now here you are," she responded, with a good amount of excitement in her voice, making it apparent that she, too, would be seeing the Eiffel Tower for the first time. "Yes," I answered emphatically, "Here I am!"

As I walked quickly across the street, I glanced to my left at the Parisian architecture that I had seen on television back home on those travel shows, with white stone walls and violet roofs; now it was unfolding before me.

I felt a bit as if I was floating when I finally reached the other side of the street.

"Stop and look," a man said to me as I scurried by. He was referring to the blanket on the ground in front of him littered with souvenirs. I was tempted as he showed me a small replica of the Tower, maybe twelve inches high, that danced with white lights with the click of a switch. "No," I said, refocusing now. "I am going to see the Eiffel Tower." He seemed unimpressed by my declaration and shoved the miniature tower toward me. "Twenty Euros."

"Not now, maybe later," I said, while walking off and without waiting for his response. Then, just a few seconds later, it came into view.

I stopped in my tracks and smiled, glancing upward at the nine-teenth-century phenomenon. This has been the ridiculously import-ant symbol of my trip. I knew that when I stood at the base of the Eiffel Tower, it would mark the official fulfillment of my dream. That photo on my vision board back in the States would no longer be something that I poured over on spring days. I would finally be living, instead of dreaming about this journey.

So the Tower and I had a special moment as I glanced upward while snapping a plethora of photos, but this was only the beginning. I was still outside the fenced area that led to the Tower; the structure was still several yards away. The real feast will be reaching the base of the tower and perhaps climbing the steps to the upper levels.

Soon I was in a line of tourists at a security booth, waiting to go through the gate to the Tower grounds. Once I cleared security, I walked slowly to the underbelly of the structure and looked up at the endless lattice structure. At that moment, something changed.

Standing under the inter-woven metal giant, and gazing upward, I felt dizzy and nearly haunted by the height and massive wrought-iron structure, towering more than one thousand feet overhead.

I was mesmerized by the vague images of people climbing the stairs to the upper levels, and an elevator that seemed to crawl upward from the ground and vanish somewhere in the shadows of the upper floors. It felt somewhat like standing in the belly of a beast, not a terrible beast, but a beast, nonetheless.

Completed in 1889, and located on the Champ de Mars, next to the River Seine, the Tower, which is the tallest building in Paris, is the architectural big baby of engineer, Gustave Eiffel. Rejected at first as a monstrosity, it has since charmed many travelers, and has become a symbol of great achievement.

The sun now setting, I hurried to take snapshots of the large gothic structure as fascinated tourists scurried around me, trying to make sense of the giant. Finally, I walked to yet another line, this time for a ticket, only ten Euros, to climb the structure on foot to the first level, some three hundred steps.

At nightfall, I took my first step on a circular climb, stopping often to catch my breath. Some twenty minutes later, breathless and tired, I reached the first observation level of the Tower and walked to the perimeter of the structure to view what I could of Paris. At that moment, the infatuation with Eiffel made sense to me—it afforded an incredible view of the City. From my little perch in front of a massive window, I could see Paris unedited.

I was met with a view of the Champs-Elysees, one of the busiest avenues in the world, with a symphony of traffic, hedged in by white lights and lovely lilac rooftops.

Then, I walked slowly around the parameters of the tower, somewhat unaware of what I might find next, feeling as if I was untying a bow on a Christmas present, and being wonderfully surprised by what's in the box—just over there, a ferry boat making its way down the River Seine, glistening in a chorus of lights! And over there, on the banks of the Seine, a melodic string of shops and cafés; and on and on, it went, with each image covered in pretty white lights.

Moments later, I pulled myself away from the spectacle and began the descent down the stairs. I tried to savor the moment realizing that this might be my one and only time at the Tower. Soon, I was walking with a crowd of other tourists through the gate, and back onto the sidewalk littered with vendors selling souvenirs.

To commemorate the moment, I paused at one vendor in particular to purchase some colorful hats laid out neatly on a piece of cloth on the ground. The vendor, a black man with a quick smile, picked one up and handed it to me. Then suddenly, an explosion of lights to my right—Eiffel lit up with what must have been a million lights from head to toe. "Oooh," I said, joined by a chorus of other tourists. It was an incredibly pleasant surprise!

I took that as my little goodbye kiss from Eiffel as I walked away with two bags full of souvenirs and a grateful heart to God that I had indeed, had the strength and found the courage to live my dream of visiting Paris.

And indeed, Paris treated me well.

What's on your vision board, your bucket list, or simply hidden in your heart that has been calling you? If not now, when? Ask God to open the door. He loves you and wants to see you live a full life.

And don't settle for less than God's best. While in Paris, on my way to the Eiffel Tower, the souvenir salesman tried to sell me a miniature version of the Tower, one around twelve inches high. Wouldn't it have been odd if I brought it and went home without seeing the actual thing that I had traveled such a far distance to see? "No," I said, "I am going to see the Eiffel Tower." I was laser focused, and what a splendid moment it turned out to be!

What great things are God calling you to do? Don't settle for the mini version. Don't settle for that relationship that's just okay, or the job that is so-so. You deserve better than that. You have greatness in you!

You can totally live out your dreams. Put your hand in His and step forward! And happy trailblazing!

The enchanting Eiffel Tower, 2019.

*I stayed in a village in Montmartre and had
tea at a little cafe near the center.*

A Trailblazer's Journey to:
JERUSALEM, ISRAEL

23

The Pilgrimage

ast year I decided to take a trip to Jerusalem. I kept my decision to myself until the day before I was about to leave because
I didn't want anyone to talk me out of it. Finally, I decided to
tell my mother. "Don't you watch the news?" she asked. No, in fact
I did not.

I didn't want anything to talk me out of this trip! Then, out
of curiosity, I looked online for travel warnings and they were enormous. Tourist stabbed to death simply for being American, and others warned that if they are mistaken for American, they might be in
danger as well, followed by a message to use caution while traveling
to Israel, especially to Jerusalem and some other areas.

So it happened that I didn't go. By the time I finished surfing
the web I was ready to unpack my suitcase and forfeit my ticket, my
heart filled with fear of what might happen to me if I travelled there
alone. I was also aware that I didn't have a word from God (I felt the
Holy Spirit's attention on that). It was simply a dream of mine to go.

A year later, and the urge to visit Jerusalem was still strong in
my heart. This time I waited on God for clearance. "Might I go
Lord? This means a lot to me. I want to pray at the Wailing Wall." As
I prayed, I felt His usual kind and thoughtful attention.

Then I felt a *warning* from the Holy Spirit. He seemed to be
saying that the time I had scheduled to go would cross my path with

some danger. *What sort of danger?* The very worse things crossed my mind.

Because of various conditions, it was an ideal time for me to travel, but now this, a warning, and from a very important Person. I decided to wait until I got to Paris to decide. I will bring it up again in prayer to see if I might get some clarity and direction. Paris would be a good launching point for a trip to Jerusalem, with the Holy City being only around four hours away on a non-stop flight.

* * * * * * *

Near the end of my trip in Paris, while sitting in my hotel room, I prayed again. Should I go? I felt as if it was an opportunity of a lifetime and I felt too that if I didn't take the trip now, that perhaps I never would. A trip to Jerusalem was one of those precious little images pasted on my vision board—a cutout of a photo I got from the internet, superimposed with a little photo of me standing next to the Wailing Wall. I saw it when I sat at my desk and glanced up at the myriad of images that comprised my dreams. But did I have the courage to go? And what danger awaits?

After struggling with the issue in prayer, I finally felt release to go. I felt in my heart that I would not be harmed, and that God would take care of me. It was a clear and strong reassurance. So with that, I booked a flight from Paris to Tel Aviv.

Once in Tel Aviv, I was in a state of heightened awareness and caution as I joined a group of other foreigners in a shared taxi to Jerusalem. The landscape was dark so as hard as I tried, I didn't see the Wailing Wall or much of anything else while the vehicle sped along the winding roads.

I only had one mission as I sat snugly between two other tourists at the back of the van—to pray at the Wall. This special Wall, also known as the Western Wall, "is an ancient limestone wall in the Old City of Jerusalem…originally…part of the…second Jewish Temple…"[17]

God says, of the original Temple, "I have chosen and consecrated this temple so that my Name may be there forever. My eyes and my heart will always be there" (2 Chronicles 7:16, NIV). That was precisely the reason I wanted to go.

* * * * * * *

Nearly an hour after leaving the airport in Tel Aviv, the driver let me off at a place called "Ethiopia Street" in the Old City. It was a narrow little road, poorly lit, and my hotel was somewhere on that road, although I had no idea where. Finally, I stumbled across a little sign with the name of the hotel in front of a house to my left, and made my way inside.

As I swung open the door, I was met by a dark entry way and steep stairwell. "Hello?" I called out, feeling like I stepped into a creepy movie. *Where is everyone? What sort of hotel is this with no reception desk and no one in sight?* I was tempted to walk out of the building but where would I go on foot in the night in a strange city?

I reasoned that maybe I should see if there was anyone upstairs. I was arriving late after all, around 9:00 p.m., so maybe the patron is asleep by now. Finally, I saw that there was a light on under the door to my right. I knocked on the door and a woman answered back.

"I am looking for the hotel," I said. "I have reservations."

"Not here." She said.

"I have reservations for a hotel at this address."

"Not here." She then opened the door and looked down at my luggage then up at me.

"Other door."

"Where?"

"Go out and go to the back."

After noticing the puzzled look on my face, she decided to show me. She led me back to the front door and pointed to a building directly behind us with a patio, some chairs, and a lit walkway. Relieved, I thanked her and headed toward the hotel—an old stone building with high ceilings, private bedrooms, and a shared bathroom.

After checking in, I was happy to lay down on the big oversized bed in my room. It hardly fazed me that everything around me was old from years of use and that the bed was unusually hard.

I was in Jerusalem, finally!

And first thing tomorrow, I will make my way to the Wailing Wall.

24

The Wailing Wall

The morning after arriving to Jerusalem, I had little precious time. I had a return flight for Paris scheduled for 5:00 a.m. the following morning, which gave me only one day to see what I could of Jerusalem. If I did nothing else, it was essential to me that I got to pray at the Wailing Wall. I was told it was only a fifteen-minute walk from the hotel, so I headed out on foot, stopping a few times to ask directions.

In my mind, I could see myself walking up to the Wall, reaching out a hand, praying and connecting with God in a way that can only happen there. I felt tired, exhausted from not sleeping well, and hungry as I headed toward the City center in the warm sun.

Before arriving at the Wall, I decided to stop and use the restroom, and as I turned in circles for signs of the place, a man called out to me.

"Do you need help?" He had sores on his mouth and was wearing dress slacks, a dress shirt and jacket.

"I'm just looking for the ladies' room," I said. At that moment I spotted it close by to my left, maybe nine or ten yards.

"Are you here with a group?" Something about him didn't seem right.

"Yes," I said, surprising myself.

"I can show you around," he said, "for little money. Three hundred shekels."

"Sorry, I can't afford that."

"Okay," he said, "Two hundred shekels."

"Sorry."

"Well," he said. "The ladies' room is right over there. We can talk when you come out."

I went into the ladies' room and stood still for a moment thinking about the man waiting outside. Then, I felt the attention of Jesus. Something was wrong! He was sending me an alarm signal and I knew He was speaking about the man with the sores on his mouth waiting just outside the door. Then, a second alarm from Jesus, just an urgency in my spirit and sensing His presence! *It's really unusual for Him to send two danger signs in a row!*

Back outside, the man came over to me as I exited the ladies' room. "Well?" he asked. "How much can you pay?"

I politely declined his services and headed in the opposite direction. Then, he began to shout: "You used me! You let me show you where the ladies' room was, and you had no intention of taking the tour! You wasted my time!"

As I walked away, I could hear him hurl insults at the top of his voice, using profanity and obscenity, with intense violence in his voice, filled with a history of rage! Finally, a man at a booth nearby called out to him, saying, "Don't do that!"

I walked away quickly as the raging man continued to yell after me.

I was flustered and shaken as I walked in the direction of the Wailing Wall. I knew enough not to argue with a raging lunatic, but still, it was the last thing in the world I wanted to happen after traveling so far and right before praying at the Wall!

When I arrived at the Wall, I felt wounded and quiet, the man's violent words still ringing in my ears. I lifted my hand and rested it on the Wall. "I'm here, Lord," I said, and a tear rolled down my cheek.

Then, I prayed. I thanked God for life, I prayed for my future, for this book (I felt the Holy Spirit's attention on that), and for whatever else He has in store for me. Then, I found a pen and scribbled the names of my family members, asking for mercy on their lives and I tucked it in one of those crevices in the Wall.

My special moment at the Wailing Wall.

As I glanced down at the ground, I noticed several pieces of paper piled in small heaps at the base of the Wall; those heartfelt prayers that had been tucked in the Wall by those like me, reaching for their God, that fell to the ground, perhaps taken by the wind. I felt sorry to see some people stepping on them or shoving them aside with their feet, and taking that as a cue, I tried very hard to find a spot in the Wall where my little list might fit smugly.

Then, I returned to my pen and on a small piece of paper, wrote a little personal message to God, of love and gratitude.

Afterward, I stood behind the line of women praying at the Wall, while studying the Wall carefully for a spot where my message might fit. Then, I saw it, over to my left, and when the lady moved from in front of me, I reached over and tucked my message in as smugly as I could.

As I stepped away, I was aware that my visit would be very short. I remembered those people I saw on television back home who talked about getting great revelations from God when they visited Jerusalem. My plane would be leaving shortly. What could happen in such a short time? I too wanted a word from God. Then, I felt God speak to my heart. "Cast all your cares on Me," He said. "Because I care for you." It was immensely personal and heartfelt, from His heart to mine. *Thank you, Lord.*

Then, as I walked away from the Wall, something incredible happened! I had a sudden revelation in my spirit of God unfolding that little prayer I had placed snugly in the Wall and reading it. (I felt the Holy Spirit's attention on that.) That was enough for me. He got my note of love and gratitude, and He had me on His mind. I was satisfied with that. I felt so fortunate that He would let me know that He got my message.

I'm glad I took the trip to Jerusalem, even though I went alone. The other option was to continue to wait more years for someone else to decide to go with me or save forever for one of those mega-expensive group tours. I also didn't want the chatter that sometimes comes with groups. There is safety in numbers, so it's a good option for most people, and I wouldn't advise traveling alone as I did without a word from God.

It was enough for me that I had clearance from God, and as startling and disturbing as it was to encounter that troubled man on the trip, it showed me that no matter what I come across, God is not far off. The Holy Spirit warned me before I started the journey that I would encounter trouble; and right before the incident, Jesus showed up to alert me of danger, and to also let me know that He was with me. God kept me safe!

* * * * * * *

At some point, while I laid my hand on the Western Wall, all the troubles of my heart quieted, and for a moment, it seemed as if God and I were the only ones that remained; a hush came over me and it became about God's love toward me and my heart reaching for Him.

That visit to the Wall was priceless, something I will always treasure as my moment with God in the Holy City.

So God answered my prayer; the one I prayed before leaving the US. "Lord, please send your angel before me to create a path of safety for me." I remembered, too, His promise to bring me back safely, and I saw Him fulfill His word (I felt Jesus's attention on that). For the rest of the day, I would relax in His promises, and try to take in as much as I could of the Holy City. Before leaving Jerusalem, there was one more thing I wanted to do.

I headed for the Via Dolorosa (the Stations of the Cross) to walk along the narrow cobble stoned streets, and experience where Jesus walked on His way to the cross. (For more information, visit Faithbridgecafe.com.)

A Trailblazer's Journey to:

BANGLADESH

25

Bangladesh

Once I saw the manifestation of my dream trip to Paris and Jerusalem, I had a new level of respect for what was possible in my walk with God, and so I looked more earnestly at those images on my vision board. They were no longer a bunch of photos held onto a two-by-three cardboard with scotch tape; this was serious business! Those images were talking to me about what I could become in the days God has given me, what could be accomplished for His Kingdom. I didn't quite know how I would go about manifesting it all, but at least I had a photo, an idea, an image.

Now, whenever I glance up from my computer, I treat each large and small photo, each word scribbled with my felt tip pen, with an undercurrent of hope. Paris and Jerusalem "blew up" everything—blew up my inhibitions and the limitations I had set for myself. It let me see that indeed, I could by the grace of God, live the life I wanted. Those journeys created momentum!

In the Paris photo on my vision board (one from the internet with a superimposed photo of me), I am sitting in a café in the center of town, surrounded by tourists and Parisians, and I look quite well and content. So in Paris, when I was actually there a week ago, I was certain to find a café, and I took several photos of me sitting at a small table outside the café, with a tiny cup of espresso. As I took the selfies, I realized I was witnessing the manifestation of one of my dreams.

Then, Jerusalem. I had a picture on my vision board of the Wailing Wall with a small photo of me superimposed onto it. And so, it was as I had envisioned, when recently, I walked up to the Wall in Jerusalem and lifted my hand in prayer.

* * * * * * *

When I sat at my desk last night and looked up at my vision board at the six major visions left unfulfilled, I asked God, "Lord, which one next? Which of these matters most to You?" Shortly after praying I felt the Holy Spirit's attention on Bangladesh.

For over a year, I've had this idea of opening an orphanage and a "floating school" in Bangladesh through my 501c3 nonprofit, Manifest Global Outreach (manifestglobaloutreach.org). Of all the visions I could reach next, that appears to be the one that is closest to God's heart (and to mine). But I know now that this *can* happen because I saw Paris and Jerusalem manifest, which in themselves were sizable for me. So Bangladesh it is.

I have learned that each vision has a price tag, a cost. It would cost me something to see the manifestation of my dreams: money, time, courage, pain, commitment, boldness, stress, and serious pushing past my lethargy and fears! And the manifestation of each vision might not be so romantic as I had hoped (I felt God's attention on that). There will be some parts that are troubling or intimidating, perhaps. With a worthwhile vision, I'll likely get some pushback—some resistance.

"Get out of fantasy land," I tell myself, "and accept the blessings and deal with the trouble" (I felt the Holy Spirit's attention on that) "that comes along with working the vision. Do the homework. Consider the costs."

Because I understand that some of the visions on my board will mean confronting darkness—such as confronting child trafficking in Bangladesh while providing a safe place for children or confronting my own sense of inadequacy—I find that some images on my board are sobering. Not every vision is a stroll in Paris, but they are all important and all incredibly relevant to me living the life God intended—of impacting the world with the gospel.

I want all my visions to glorify God and His Kingdom. If there is anything on my vision board that doesn't do that, then my prayer is that God would give me understanding that I might remove it.

Yesterday, as I went about my day, I came across one singular message: "Ask God for big things." It just so happens I came across it twice from two different sources. So, Lord, I am asking for an orphanage and school in Bangladesh that has a major impact on ending child trafficking, that effectively pulls children from the streets (I felt the Holy Spirit's attention on that) and places them in a safe shelter that introduces the gospel and saves lives.

The manifestation of this vision is some time in the future and will require courage. This will require the hand of God; but I've learned through my journeys to the "far side of the world," as scribbled in the pages of this book, that no matter where I find myself, God is not far off, and that with Him all things are possible. (See Matthew 19:26.)

I learned too that no weapon forged against me can prosper; that as I trust my life to His hands, He is faithful and capable of weaving a life for me that I would not otherwise have dared to ask or think.

He is God the Father. He is God the Holy Spirit. He is God the Son. He is merciful and kind and effective in all He does; and His plans are good, to give each one of us a future and a hope! (See Jeremiah 29:11.)

In the name of Jesus, dear Reader, God bless you on your trail as you honor Him. Put Him first. Seek first His Kingdom, and then watch and see what wonderous dreams you and Him can accomplish together!

You have greatness in you! Now move forward with God! (I felt the Holy Spirit's attention on that.)

God bless you.

"Love the Lord your God with all your heart and with all your soul and with all your mind" (Matthew 22:37, NIV). Because that's how He loves you: with all His heart and with all His soul and with all His mind.

A Trailblazer's Journey to:

THE LAND
OF DREAMS
AND VISIONS

26

War of the Worlds

I had an amazing dream one night that life as I knew it on earth suddenly ended! It was one of the oddest dreams I've ever had! I kept editing it out of this book, but as I was praying at around 4:00 a.m.one day, this story, this chapter, flashed across my mind.

During prayer, I actually suggested that it not be included because it's so odd and intense and because I don't understand all the symbolism, but I felt in my heart as if God preferred for it to be included. Now, here it is:

> I dreamt that a woman was in a dressing room getting ready to marry. Four men waited outside in the parlor, just outside her dressing room door. One was handsome with dark hair and arrogant. The other three were quite ordinary looking and humble. The woman planned to choose one of them as her groom.
>
> When she stepped out of her dressing room, the ordinary humble men understood from the way she looked at them that she would not be choosing any of them. She decided to marry the handsome arrogant man.

Later, she went searching for her groom-to-be and found him standing outside on the porch. As she walked over to him, but before they could speak, she followed an urge to look up.

There in the sky, right above their heads, she saw a foreign vessel—a large Hindenburg-like ship drifting ten miles or so from the ground. It was massive and stark looking, a grey or putrid beige color, and carried with it a sort of morbid feeling.

"What's going on?'" the woman asked the handsome arrogant man. When he turned to look in her direction, she saw for the first time that he was evil. He was filled with the look of a soul-less demonic being.

"It's happening again,'" he said in disgust! He seemed to be referring to the air vessel above his head and what would happen next.

Then, the woman began running for her life from the blimp warships. She saw the ships float over the city as large barn sized doors opened on the side of the blimp, and open-top military jeeps rolled out of the vessel onto the ground. The jeeps were armed with white soldiers who began shooting everyone in sight.

The woman lived on the other side of town. She was running through the street trying to get home. The blimps were everywhere, and men from the blimps, traveling in the jeeps, were driving through the streets shooting everyone.

The woman came to a house at the bottom of a hilly street and went inside and found a young white man with light brown hair. He didn't seem surprised to see her standing there in the doorway, frantic. He seemed strangely calm. She asked him if he would lend her one of his cars for she had noticed two outside. He said he would lend her the better of the two but then changed his mind and loaned her the worse of the two. She was grateful nonetheless and promised to return it.

He handed her the car key, and she ran from the house and went running toward the car which was now parked at the top of the hilly street. As she hurried toward the top of the hill, the soldiers in the jeep turned onto the street and drove toward her. All she could think to do was to play dead. She saw cement steps nearby at the base of the hill, hurried over, and quickly laid down on the steps. "Jesus," she whispered...

Then I woke.

If the Faith-Bridge Café were an actual brick and mortar café, and we were seated at one of the tables; this would be the moment when you would see me staring into my coffee. I'm not sure which direction to go with this one. *Grant me wisdom and insight please, Lord, I pray.*

This is my spin: The horrific scenes in the dream are impossible for a nation that is covered by God! (See Psalm 9:10, Isaiah 41:10, and Nahum 1:7) So then I must conclude that the dream represents a nation in which God's hand had lifted and enemies were able to breach its borders! (See Isaiah 60:12.)

In the dream, the blimps seemed like large helium balloons floating in a clear sky, but perhaps they could have represented military subs in the blue sea. In any case, it was an invasion from a foreign nation.

The dream seems to demonstrate that the world is asleep to the dangers that surround it and therefore make choices that are very shallow and lack insight. For example, the woman in the dream was so focused on marrying and getting a handsome husband that she was totally oblivious to the fact that the man she had chosen was dangerous, even demonic, and that her world was about to be destroyed! God was not in the equation.

On the outside, her groom looked good to her—tall, charming, great hair, and smile—but underneath, he was a scoundrel! Her spiritual eyes were shut! He was trouble standing in front of her, but she couldn't see it, or didn't want to see it, until it could be hidden no longer.

She was also unaware that foreign warships were at the border, even while she planned her wedding. The Bible warns us to not be carnally minded! "Be alert and of sober mind. Your enemy the devil prowls around like a roaring lion looking for someone to devour" (1 Peter 5:8, NIV).

> For to be carnally minded is death, but to be spiritually minded is life and peace. Because the carnal mind is enmity against God; for it is not subject to the law of God, neither indeed can be. So then they that are in the flesh cannot please God. (Romans 8:6–8, KJV)

So, the woman in the dream was "carnally minded"! It was about her, the wedding day, and getting a good-looking groom! It was a form of idolatry. She failed to stay alert, and she failed to keep her mind on God. Her lack of attention to the things of God made her blind to all the dangers at hand.

* * * * * * *

I am sure that God cares and that He is merciful; so for those reading this, what can we do? God gives the answer: "If My people, who are called by Name, will humble themselves and pray and seek My face and turn from their wicked ways, then I will hear from heaven, and will forgive their sin and heal their land" (2 Chronicles 7:14, NIV). That scripture is important whether the dream is purely symbolic or an actual warning of pending danger. Seek God's face, turn from sinful choices and pray.

God is inviting us back to Himself! He has His hand outstretched (just had a vision of this).

> Seek the Lord while he may be found; call on him while he is near. (Isaiah 55:6, NIV)

> And God said, "You will seek me and find me when you seek me with all your heart." (Jeremiah 29:13, NIV)

A Trailblazer's Journey to:
The 12th Hour

27

The Debutante

So today I stepped into a bookstore to do a bit of reading. I had my own book with me (actually the manuscript that I had bound together by hand and glued on a cover). While at the bookstore, as I browsed the many professional, glossy, wonderfully designed covers of the books on the shelves, I started to wonder how my book might look on a shelf.

Then, it occurred to me to go to someone in management and see if it might be okay for me to take my humble book and put it on one of their shelves, next to the published books, and take a picture.

I felt elated at the thought and a bit silly, but I went up to a well poised young woman with straight brown hair and olive complexion, with a key dangling from her arm.

"Do you work here?" I asked before springing my request.

"Yes, I do," she said, as I struggled with the best way to ask her.

"I wrote a book," I started, "and I was wondering if it would be okay if I put it on one of the bookshelves in the store and take a picture, as a sort of inspiration, so that I can imagine it on the shelves."

"Oh, I don't think I've ever had a request like that. Let me check," she said. Then, she turned to a man standing nearby talking to a patron. He may have been in his late thirties, and had the air of an avid reader indeed, quite professorial. Motioning to me, she said,

"She was just wondering if she could take a picture of her book on the shelves."

"Of course," He said without hesitating, then went on speaking to the patron.

I asked the woman to follow me to the bookshelf because it would involve taking my book from my bag, putting it on one of the shelves, taking a picture, and then removing it from the shelf and placing it back into my bag. I was sure that would look odd to security.

"Where do you want to take the picture," she asked, seeming a little adventerous herself.

"Ahm, the inspirational section." I hadn't really thought about it before, but it seemed the right section for a book on never giving up, trusting God, and faith.

Seconds later we were standing somewhere near the back center of the store and I was placing my little book next to the well polished books.

As I foucssed my phone camera on the tattered cover, I noticed the scracthed up edges where I had folded it by hand and pulled off some of the ink accidentaly. I noticed too that it had trouble standing up because the cover was a bit too large for the inside pages. In anycase, it was my baby and it was standing there, for the first time, on the shelf, to the glory of a loving and patient God who labored with me to this point, with a long way left to go.

I took three pictures, straigtnening the book up when it started to droop to the right. Then, I thanked the young woman. She was kind enough to give me a business card as I was leaving, and told me to be in touch when I was ready to get the book on the shelves, for real this time, and she wished me luck.

So *Courageous* got its first outing today. She was the akward looking debutante at the ball, but she was at the ball nonethelsess, even if but for a moment.

As I type this, I'm on my fourth draft and pray it might be ready in August. I'm so grateful that God would use me for this writing project, that He would show me how to turn the broken limbs of my life into something useful (I felt the Holy Spirit's attention on this).

God is wonderful, period. Full stop. He won't let you down!

7/21/18 11:18 p.m.

When I felt called to write this book, I just started and it took years, but by the grace of God, I kept at it. I prayed and wrote. The more I wrote, the stronger in the Lord I became. It was a journey that strengthened my faith, glory to God (I felt the Holy Spirit's attention on this).

I am now looking at what I believe is near the final draft. So now I have to get it to you somehow. And hopefully, you will find the love of God in these pages.

* * * * * * *

Are you ready to step out in faith for the sake of the gospel of Jesus Christ? Bring your appetite for adventure and join the conversation at Faithbridgecafe.com.

28

The Twelfth Hour

Some years ago, I visited the Jerusalem Center in New Jersey, a church led by Rabbi Jonathan Cahn. Many know Rabbi Cahn for his New York Times best seller, *The Harbinger*. While at his church one day, I asked him to autograph my copy of his book; and I took the opportunity to ask him to pray for my ministry, which he graciously did.

It just so happens that Rabbi Cahn's *The Harbinger* was the original inspiration for this book. Cahn's message was repentence and turning to God, and it inspired me to begin my own journey of reflection and a more committed walk with God.

Now, a decade after meeting the Messianic Rabbi, I understand that God is willing to use anyone who will live a life of repentence and submission to His word and direction. (I felt the Holy Spirit's attention on this.) God uses broken vessels like me, and if God can use me, He can use anyone.

* * * * * * *

I only wanted to tell you, in all of this work, that Jesus saves! (I felt the Holy Spirit's attention on this.) "For whosoever calls upon the name of the Lord shall be saved" (Romans 10:13, KJV). All the chapters in this book point to that one fact! "'For I know the plans

I have for you,' declares the Lord, 'plans to prosper you and not to harm you, plans to give you hope and a future'" (Jeremiah 29:11, NIV). Jesus is at the center of that plan!

When someone says "yes," to God and truly surrender to His will for their life, God shows up and shows Himself strong on their behalf. And that's what this book has been about.

Has God put it on your heart to serve Him in ministry? Have you felt inspired to write a book, to make a movie, to build a school, to share the gospel?

Trailbalzer, it's the twelfth hour! Step out and live the life you've always wanted. Receive God's best for you! There will be challenges, but those will only make you stronger as you remain prayerful and trust in Him!

Blaze a new trail. If only you knew how much God cares about you! Move forward knowing, "Everything is possible for one who believes" (Mark 9:23, NIV). If God has called you to blaze a trail for the sake of the gospel, then take that leap of faith. Step out!

* * * * * *

It has been an honor to have you on this segment of the journey. If I could leave you with one word, it would be God loves you! (I felt Jesus's attention on this.) That drives everything He does! Whatever you are going through, whatever is confronting you, take courage. Trust Jesus as your savior. Find peace.

God bless you as you serve Him. If you have yet to say the "sinner's prayer" to experience amazing salvation in Jesus, here is one more opportunity:

Prayer of Salvation

"Dear Lord Jesus, I know I am a sinner, and I ask for your forgiveness. I believe you died for my sins and rose from the dead. I trust and follow you as my Lord and Savior. Guide my life and help me to do your will. In your name, amen."[18]

> God so loved the world that he gave his one
> and only Son, that whoever believes in him shall
> not perish but have eternal life. (John 3:16, NIV)

JESUS SAVES

A Trailblazer's Journey to:

THE KINGDOM
OF GOD

29

The Kingdom of God

Introduction

If I had to give up everything in this book except for one section, this is the one I would keep. This was the purpose for my journey, even my reason for living (I felt the Holy Spirit's attention on that). It wasn't Japan, Jamaica, Paris, Jerusalem, or the USA—as amazing as those places are—they were simply doors that led me to this moment in time.

The Kingdom of God is the central message of Jesus's ministry. He told the crowds, "I must proclaim the good news of the kingdom of God... because that is why I was sent" (Luke 4:43, NIV). In keeping with this mission, He preached the Kingdom wherever He went, using this parable: "[T]he kingdom of heaven is like a treasure hidden in a field. When a man found it, he hid it again, and in his joy, he went and sold all he had and bought that field" (Matthew 13:45–46, NIV).

"Jesus presented another parable to them. 'The kingdom of heaven is like a man who sowed good seed in his field'" (Matthew 13:24, NIV). But He didn't just tell about the Kingdom; His announcement was followed by incredible demonstrations of Kingdom power! Blind eyes were opened (see Mark 10:46–52), and people were even raised from the dead (see John 11:38–44).

The Kingdom was manifesting in ways people had never seen before, and it was shifting and saving lives—bringing healing, hope, and purpose for living. This was unlike any kingdom anyone had ever imagined or experienced!

Now, I am beginning to understand why Jesus urges people to seek first the Kingdom of God (see Matthew 6:33) because the Kingdom holds the *keys* to successful Christian living (I feel the Holy Spirit's attention on this), and that is why this particular section is the heart of this book.

* * * * * * *

I felt God's presence throughout this writing process, and especially in this section. Sometimes, it was as if God was standing by my side and coaching me on what to write and giving me the courage to be candid, to be transparent. At the moments when I felt God's attention, I shared the occasion with the reader.

So when I write: "I felt the Holy Spirit's attention on that" or "I felt God's attention on that," or even, "I felt Jesus's attention on that," I am flagging those moments of special encouragement, support, and guidance.

God is truly committed to helping me (and the readers on this journey) to understand and learn (I felt the Holy Spirit's attention on that) about His Kingdom.

God is willing to teach anyone who is willing to study the subject. In scripture God says, "I will instruct you and teach you… I will guide you with My eye" (Psalm 32:8, NKJV). And in another place in scripture, Jesus says, "the Holy Spirit, whom the father will send… will teach you all things" (John 14:26, NIV). Also, "when the Spirit of truth comes, he will guide you into all truth" (John 16:13, NIV).

* * * * * * *

As I worked on this section, sometimes I felt unsure of myself. I kept asking God, "Are you sure I should be doing this? There are lots of more capable people out there." Yet believing I don't need to be a

Bible scholar to get the basics of the Kingdom of God (I felt the Holy Spirit's attention on this), I decided to take the journey.

Still, I needed His reassurance. "Might I have a word, Lord?" I prayed. Whenever I ask to hear God's word on a matter, He always responds. So I waited, and within an hour or so, I received: "God wouldn't allow it if you didn't have what it takes."

So I continue this journey believing God will help me, that He will hold my right hand and lead me forward.

As I studied for this section, I found a variety of opinions and interpretations about the Kingdom of God. In the end, I just did what made sense within the context of what I saw in scripture.

Finally, this section is not meant to be exhaustive or exhausting. It is merely an *introduction* to the Kingdom (I felt the Holy Spirit's attention on this).

> And this gospel of the kingdom will be preached in all the world as testimony to all nations, and then the end will come. (Matthew 24:14, NIV)

There is an added benefit to leaning in and studying this topic. Your spirit will become more "tuned" to the presence of God. So if you've had difficulty hearing from God or discerning His voice (I felt the Holy Spirit's attention on this), then draw near to His Kingdom (I felt Jesus's attention on this), and there you will find Him.

As you read through this section, don't rely solely on what I've found; study for yourself (and you are invited to share your ideas, questions, and insights at faithbridgecafe.com).

30

The King and His Kingdom

On February 21, 2018, I had a sudden revelation that God was near. It was the sort of impression a child gets when a loving parent walks into a room—there is an immediate spirit to Spirit connection; but this time was different than the others. I felt as if God was "physically" walking among us, as if He descended to earth.

The revelation was so striking, my first thought was, "Why is the Father here?" I meant, why is He here in such a prominent way? What is happening in the earth; what's transpiring?

It may have been later that day when I heard the news that Billy Graham died. The world-famous evangelist of the gospel of Jesus Christ was now transitioning to Heaven. I began to wonder if God came down to earth to see to that transition Himself; the way He did at the death of Moses, that great man of God who died in Moab. (See Deuteronomy 34.)

Somehow, it made sense that a God who treasures those who live faithfully before Him (I felt God's attention on that) might very well descend to earth to see to the transition of one of His servants. And that may very well had been the case, but perhaps there's more.

* * * * * * *

Before Dr. Graham died, some prophetic circles predicted[19] that after his death, there would be an acceleration toward the end of times. In other words, his death would mark the beginning of one of the toughest moments in history as we move quickly toward the end of days.

Indeed, since his death, world events have spiraled out of control. There has been an acceleration of troubles—the world was recently hit with several intense disasters at once—from COVID-19 to worldwide economic collapse to global civil unrest! The chaos reminds us that the end is near!

So maybe God is here in a mightier way (I felt the Holy Spirit's attention on that) to usher in the return of Christ. And as we draw closer to His return, the "signs" of the end times are converging and accelerating.

In a prophetic word on a TBN broadcast,[20] Dr. Mark Chironna said, "We are coming into perhaps the most significant day in church history, and there are a number of things that are going to begin to converge."[21] (I felt God's attention on that.)

"[T]here is gonna be a convergence of the signs...an acceleration..."[22] (I felt God's attention on the last part that sentence.)

"Things are going to begin to overlap."[23] (I felt God's attention on that.) "And when that happens...the earth is going to see a 21st century manifestation of the demonstration of the Spirit..."[24] (I felt the Holy Spirit's attention on that.)

* * * * * * *

In Luke chapter 21, Jesus warned about the chaotic times that would precede His return, saying:

> [25]There will be signs in the sun and moon and stars, and on the earth dismay among the nations...
> [26]Men will faint from fear and anxiety over what is coming upon the earth, for the powers of the heavens will be shaken.

And, He offered this word of encouragement:

> [27]At that time they will see the Son of Man coming in a cloud with power and great glory. [28]When these things begin to happen, stand up and lift up your heads, because your redemption is drawing near...

Then, He included this warning:

> [34]But watch yourselves, or your hearts will be weighed down by dissipation, drunkenness, and the worries of life—and that day will spring upon you suddenly like a snare...[36]pray that you may have the strength to escape all that is about to happen and to stand before the son of Man. (Luke 21: 25-36, Berean Study Bible)

Earth is filled with worry and anxiety right now; with people trying to numb themselves to all that's happening around them, but Jesus tells us to do just the opposite—to gird up and pray and stay focused! Jesus said, pray "to have the strength to escape" the chaos and to stand before Him.

* * * * * * *

The Bible warns us to be ready for days like these—when the King comes upon us suddenly and His Kingdom manifest in ways like we have never seen before. (See Luke 17:26–27.) As I searched for scripture on this topic, I felt God's attention on that verse in Luke, which states, "And just as it happened in the days of Noah, so it will be also in the days of the Son of Man ..." (Luke 17:26). (I felt Jesus's attention on this. I felt the Holy Spirit's attention on this.)

"They were eating, they were drinking, they were marrying, they were being given in marriage, until the day that Noah entered the ark, and the flood came and destroyed them all" (Luke 17:26–27, NASB).

* * * * * * *

So, how do we not be oblivious to the move of God in this current age but be mindful of His presence and be aware of how He is working in the earth?

How do we not get distracted by money or high-end gadgets but honor Him with our lives?

Jesus gave us the answer. He tells anyone who will listen to seek first the Kingdom of God (see Matthew 6:33). By being "Kingdom minded," one becomes connected to the move of God in the earth. That connection is lifesaving (I felt God's attention on this) because it is a door to relationship with God—to Him including you in His end time plans—to salvation in Jesus, the Christ.

In other words, if you realize yourself as a citizen of the Kingdom of God through the new birth experience in Jesus, the Christ, then you will also realize your role in the end times (I felt the Holy Spirit's attention on this).

A Kingdom connection is the key to living the life God had always intended for you to live, and we are running out of time (I felt the Holy Spirit's attention on this). So that connection is more critical than ever (I felt the Holy Spirit's attention on this).

Kingdom-mindfulness is the way to live a life free of shipwrecking-sin; of keeping your attention on God in these last days!

A sense of purpose and righteousness, and a proper alignment with the move of God—all of that is found in the Kingdom (I felt the Holy Spirit's attention on this).

So I am doing what seems prudent, and by taking this journey with me, you are as well: to study, pray, and learn more about God and His Kingdom.

An opportunity to draw near to God, to study, and to seek His Kingdom is at hand.

This is an open window, but time is short.

31

Time is Short

When I last saw Justin, he had that smile I had become accustomed to. He was trying to put me at ease, trying to help me deal with the sight of his frail body, lying helplessly in the narrow bed, with a remote control sitting near his hand. I tried to explain why it took me so long to visit, then turned my attention to the plastic bag with the brown gruel hanging from a pole near his bed. His nutrients, I came to understand, but his body was rejecting it.

I thought back to last year when he first became ill. I, and many others, prayed for him regularly, and asked God to have mercy and help him to recover. After several months of chemotherapy and weight loss, he *did* recover. Praise God! But then something amazing happened. He returned to his old habits—he still drank beers and craved cake and treats from the donut shop. He seemed to hate fruits and vegetables and relished protein, starches and processed foods.

I remember going to his home and taking fruits and vegetables and begging him to eat healthy. He shrugged it off, laughed, and tried to reassure me that he had everything under control. His body was thin, and he looked tired from months of chemo. *He needs to make different choices; why isn't he listening?* Sometimes he did try to change, mostly to please his family, but then he would slip back into old habits.

One day, as he reclined in front of the TV in his home, I asked him the same question I had asked on other occasions. "Do you want me to pray for you?" I felt it was the one thing that could turn his life around; the one thing that could open his eyes to the way his choices were affecting his life. He laughed and shook his head no. He seemed confident that he could handle his recovery without God and seemed to think prayer was silly.

He also refused to go to therapy to help his body regain its strength. Within months, the cancer returned, and he was back in the hospital, in the intensive care unit.

He needed a trachea to drain the fluid from his lungs and was being fed through a tube in his stomach. He listened as the doctor told him that he had only one year to live, and he wept.

He wanted to eat, but he couldn't at that point because he had no strength to swallow. He would have gladly eaten a grapefruit, or drank some spring water, but his body was shutting down. The doctors worked to create some sort of chance for recovery, using the best they had in their knowledge base to give him a fighting chance.

Frustrated by the fact that he didn't heed the warnings from his family and the doctors to take better care of himself, I went back to God and prayed. "Give him another chance, Lord, to recover. Let him see more years and not just the one year the doctor predicted. Please give Him more time to accept Jesus as Lord and turn his life around."

After praying, I had a vision of him returning home and beginning to eat again without the feeding tube. I knew it was probably just wishful thinking, but it gave me hope. I took it as a sign that perhaps God had answered my prayers. It would be a pure act of mercy (I felt Jesus's attention on this).

In the weeks that followed, he only grew worse, until one day, surrounded by family and doctors, his physician who had labored with him up till then told him that they were considering discontinuing treatment and putting him on hospice care. At that moment, he lost it; all composure left him, and he wept. "The devil is taking me down!" he said. "The devil is taking me down!" In the following days, his health seemed to be spinning further out of control. He spent his days in the ICU hooked up to wires and tubes. It looked like his fight, all enthusiasm for life, had left him. In the natural, he looked hopeless.

I too, began to doubt. My biggest concern was the fact that he had lost his power of speech. The family was willing to re-approach him for the hundredth time perhaps, with the notion of accepting Jesus as Lord, but now he couldn't confess; he couldn't speak. He would have to say it in his heart, and that would have to be enough. As he laid in ICU, he didn't want to see anyone, except a few family members.

If only I could help him to focus on Jesus; but how do I get the salvation message before his eyes? Then, while walking through a store, I saw the answer. It was a yellow rubber duckie sitting in a pile of rubber duckies in the children's section. I purchased it, took it home and used a marker to write his name on the duck's forehead, and "Jesus Saves" across the duck's chest. It looked ridiculous, but it would get his attention. It might even make him smile.

I don't know how he reacted when his wife took him the duckie, but it was reported back to me that it was placed in an area of his hospital room where he had a clear view of it at all times. I continued to pray and left the rest to God.

A week or so later, one of my other relatives stood by his bed and took another shot at the prayer of salvation. She told him God was his only hope now, that he needed to trust God. "Ask Jesus to forgive you for your sins and to help you," she told him. Unable to speak, he nodded at her words.

The devil won't take him down! That's my confession. My prayer. (I felt God's attention on this.)

* * * * * * *

The event made me examine my own life. I developed appreciation for the fact that we are all just passing through life; that it is a huge privilege to live, to be able to have conversations, drive, eat, sit up and walk by the sea, and pray, while others are in hospitals hooked up to machines. Life is opportunity and no one promises us tomorrow; it is by the grace of God that we breathe and move and have our being (see Acts 17:28). Such a huge blessing that we take it for granted because it flows to most of us so easily. But do we value God's blessing? Do we listen when He speaks? Do we heed his warnings? He speaks to help us avoid shipwrecking our lives.

The warning might be to change one's lifestyle, or to get out of a bad relationship. It most certainly is to accept Jesus as Lord (I felt the Holy Spirit's attention on this) while there is still time. To turn from sin and receive everlasting life! To not wait until disaster strikes!

The issue for most of us is that we are slow to comply. (I felt God's attention on this.) Often times, we wait until the bottom collapses and the blessing is pulling away from us before we pay attention.

Perhaps all of us have been guilty of slow compliance in some area of life. Slow compliance might be due to our own stubbornness, or it might be some sort of spiritual warfare—something blocking the truth from our eyes—or fear of the unknown or simply a reluctance for change. So God sends people to try to "wake" us up, to warn us of pending danger.

Whatever the case, God urges us to listen!

Update: Five minutes ago, I got the news that Justin (not his actual name) passed away this morning. I will remember his kind smile, and his nod at the words during the prayer of salvation as he laid in his hospital bed, unable to speak. I trust he listened. I trust he heard. I believe God saved. (I felt Jesus's attention on this.)

(I felt the Holy Spirit's attention on this.)

Prayer of Salvation

"Dear Lord Jesus, I know I am a sinner, and I ask for your forgiveness. I believe you died for my sins and rose from the dead. I trust and follow you as my Lord and Savior. Guide my life and help me to do your will. In your name, amen."[25]

* * * * * * *

Life is opportunity. Let's not waste time. (I felt the Holy Spirit's attention on this.) The Kingdom of God is at hand.

32

Kingdom of God

Opportunity

I grew up in a poor village in Jamaica. One day, my older sister was running through the bush and stepped on a rusty sardine can. Her life changed after that moment! She developed a massive infection—polio and paralysis on one side. So when my mother had opportunity to move to the USA, she saw it as a chance to give her daughters a better life.

US citizenship opened up a world of possibilities for us. My older sister got medical care that we could never afford on the island, and she got married and had children. Her life might have turned out quite differently in our small house on the Jamaican hillside without running water and electricity.

The calamity my sister experienced on the island was troubling, but it forced us to reach for options that we might not have considered were we comfortable with our circumstances. We reached for something outside the little island world that we knew, and that association created new opportunities for us.

* * * * * *

Perhaps you're not living on an island, and maybe you're not living in physical poverty, but you can relate to wanting more out of life, for wanting life with purpose and a sense of security about your future. Life might be feeling a bit tiring and maybe even boring. Or perhaps you know perfectly well what it's like to *not* know where the next meal is coming from.

Whatever the situation, the Kingdom of God provides a fascinating opportunity to reach outside the limited world we know by providing a solution to our spiritual *and* physical poverty. The solution is the innovative and incredibly powerful new birth experience—a radical change that involves "birth" into the Kingdom of God as citizens and members of God's household (see Ephesians 2:19).

So now, for those who recognize that they are poor and in need of salvation, poverty creates opportunity—a chance to reach higher (I felt the Holy Spirit's attention on that) for a solution that can radically transform your life.

Kingdom citizenship opens a spiritual dimension that has massive benefits, including eternal life; but it's not just about living forever, as fascinating as that is. It's about living good-quality eternal life, finding one's purpose, and finding a life packed with meaning.

And there is something else: Every Kingdom citizen is born in the *image* of God. How incredible is that and what wealth of possibilities does that present? (I felt the Holy Spirit's attention on that.)

So how do we access this Kingdom? It starts by admitting spiritual poverty, by asking for help. Jesus then offers the solution (I felt the Holy Spirit's attention on that) by providing a door into the Kingdom. This act of grace takes the form of a born-again experience.

Then as Kingdom citizens, more becomes possible. Our earthly life of limitations and anxiety now has a different tone, a different destiny, as the fascinating world we live in becomes the intriguing Kingdom of God.

We have the privilege of coming under the authority and rule of an incredibly powerful King who manages to overflow with compassion, love, and patience (see 1 John 4:7–21).

* * * * * * *

So what is the Kingdom of God and why is it so important to our well-being? Here are seven points about the Kingdom:

First, the Kingdom of God is a powerful empire! "A kingdom is a country, state, or territory ruled by a king or queen."[26]

The Kingdom of God is ruled by an incredibly powerful King known as the God of Abraham. His Kingdom is massive and encompasses the entire universe!

Part of understanding the Kingdom of God is understanding how a kingdom operates on earth. Let's take a look at Britain—otherwise known as the United Kingdom of Great Britain and Northern Ireland (UK)—as one example of kingdom living.

The UK has London, England, as the central headquarters (capital).[27] It is a constitutional monarchy[28] with a currently reigning Queen Elizabeth II.

> A constitutional monarchy is a form of government in which a monarch...acts as the head of state within the parameters of a written or unwritten constitution...Constitutional monarchies are the opposite of absolute monarchies, in which the monarch holds all power over the government and the people...[29]

So while the queen of England is confined in her power to rule by the written constitution and a parliamentary ruling body, God of the Kingdom is not limited in scope of power to rule. He is an absolute Monarch with total reign and rule.

> Absolute monarchy is a form of government in which the monarch exercises ultimate governing authority...his...powers are not limited by a constitution or by the law. An absolute monarch wields unrestricted political power over the sovereign state and its people.[30]

In other words, God is a real King with a throne in a real place. His Kingdom is expansive and unlimited, and His power to rule is absolute.

The capital[31] of any kingdom is where the king has his throne; therefore, the Kingdom of God has Heaven as central headquarters. Scripture tells us that "The Lord is in His holy temple; the Lord is on His heavenly throne…" (Psalm 11:4; see also Isaiah 66:1).

Second, the Kingdom of God is not a religion. As one author states, "Religion is what man does until he finds the kingdom…Religion wants to escape the earth, the Kingdom impacts, influences, and changes earth."[32]

The Kingdom of God is here with the mission of saving everyone on earth by bringing a struggling humanity in line with salvation, by eradicating sin, and by making Kingdom citizenship possible! It is not here to form a religion; it is here to impact the earth with the wisdom of God and delivering power of the Holy Spirit!

The Kingdom of God is therefore not a religious institution—it is a massive and powerful Empire! It was not contrived by man; it flows from God! It provides power tools that will enable you to live an overcoming life on earth!

Third, God's word is law. In a "true" kingdom, whatever the king says is the law of the kingdom. So laws are not adopted by popular vote; rather, they are established by the word of the king. Concerning God's word, scripture states: "All your words are true, all your righteous laws are eternal" (Psalm 119:160, NIV).

Because God's words become the law of the Kingdom, no one can change it. So even though a political leader or a religious leader on earth might vote to adopt laws contrary to the word of God, it is outside the Kingdom of God and doesn't apply within the Kingdom.

The Kingdom of God is congruent and consistent and won't contradict itself. God is unwavering and clear concerning the laws of His Kingdom.

The Kingdom rules and standards are high and nonnegotiable and are found in the Bible.

Fourth, the Kingdom of God is a holy place. In the Kingdom of God, all power to rule lies with God Himself—an absolute monarch—and He has spoken concerning sin. Because sin is destructive and runs contrary to life, God has determined that sin is illegal in His Kingdom. God totally opposes sin (but not the sinner).

God opposes sin because sin springs from satan's kingdom of darkness, and because sin is a tool used by satan to tear down humanity. (See 1 John 3:4. See also Romans 5:12.) So He condemns sin in every form because sin separates people from the Kingdom.

The Bible is the constitution of the Kingdom of God; it tells us what God offers the citizens of His Kingdom and what He expects of us. He expects every Kingdom citizen to repent of sin and to avoid acts that lead to death and decay, for example.

According to the Bible:

> [S]exual immorality, impurity and debauchery; idolatry and witchcraft; hatred, discord, jealousy, fits of rage, selfish ambition, dissensions, factions and envy; drunkenness, orgies, and the like. I warn you, as I did before, that those who live like this will not inherit the kingdom of God. (Galatians 5:19–21, NIV)

And in another place, it says:

> Do you not know that the unrighteous will not inherit the kingdom of God? Do not be deceived. Neither fornicators, nor idolaters, nor adulterers, nor homosexuals, nor sodomites, nor thieves, nor covetous, nor drunkards, nor revilers, nor extortioners will inherit the kingdom of God. And such were some of you. But you were washed, but you were sanctified, but you were justified in the name of the Lord Jesus and by the Spirit of our God. (1 Corinthians 6:9–11, NKJV)

God doesn't condone sin as a lifestyle in His Kingdom. It doesn't mean that the believer never sins, but the heart of the believer is to repent and align with the word of God, and God provides help to those who want to repent through the power of the Holy Spirit. (See John 16:13 and John 16:18.)

God doesn't force compliance but gives people the power to choose. He says, "I have set before you life and death, blessings and curses. Now choose life, so that you and your children may live and that you may love the Lord your God, listen to his voice, and hold fast to him. For the Lord is your life..." (Deuteronomy 40:19–20, NIV). To choose God and His Kingdom is to choose life.

If you have sin in your life when you come to Christ, He will *welcome* you with the objective of *helping* you to release sin and live a life worthy of your royal calling (I sense the devil is troubled by that sentence). Jesus will accept you where you are! You don't have to "get right" before accepting Jesus as Lord. Accepting Jesus as Lord will help you to get on track with choices that bless your life (I felt the Holy Spirit's attention on this).

The opportunity to be born into the Kingdom of God as a citizen of that great empire will radically transform your life!

Fifth, the Kingdom of God is love forward. I read a true story once about a fireman who was responding to a blazing fire that went out of control, devastating everything in its path. After putting out the fire, he took a walk through the charred woods, a once lively green space, now flattened by the blaze. Suddenly, he came across a majestic bird with a huge wingspan, lying belly down on the ground.

The bird, with its wings extended, was dead, having been burnt up by the fire. The fireman thought it strange that such a great bird with massive wings didn't take flight to safety. Curious, he gave the dead bird a nudge with his foot; and when he did, several chicks scurried out from under the wings. The bird let itself be burnt alive so that the chicks might survive. Radical! Yet that's the love of the Father! That's Jesus on the cross, completely sacrificial with nothing to gain, while those under His covering has everything to gain.

You see, it's a love thing. Not a judgment thing. God is going through all that He goes through because He wants you to live, not die. He loves the world. That's why He sent Jesus to pay the penalty for our sins (see John 3:16).

That's why Jesus stretched his arms out on a cross, took the beating, the nails, the crown of thorns, took the time in hell for three days and three nights, took your sins and my sins in his own body, so that we might survive! He triumphed over death so that the world might not be destroyed by sin (see 1 Peter 2:24).

He, in effect, stretches His "wings" over us.

So in the firefighter story, what if one of the chicks refused to be covered? The chick didn't quite understand the magnitude of the problem and decided to wiggle out from under the protective wings and go his own way in the woods. That's the dilemma. How does God get across to people that, from His perspective, there is a fire kindling, and to take shelter under the "wings" of Jesus?

Those who stay complacent remain under the devil's dark rule and have the same fate as the devil because the devil and his dark little empire is sinking. The devil's strategy is to not go down to hell alone rather to pull as many people down as possible. But now that the Kingdom of God is here, now that Jesus is here, everyone has a choice because Jesus brings delivering power by covering us with His wings, all the while being motivated by God's love for humanity (I felt the Holy Spirit's attention on that).

Sixth, the Kingdom of God is a welcoming place. You can approach the throne of God as a citizen of His Kingdom and as a child of God.

Being a child of God takes a little getting used to. First, you are born into a royal family, into a monarchy, whose leader just happens to be God, your Father.

How do you stay mindful that He is King and live life with all its ups and downs and mistakes and go to Him as a child who needs direction? How do you juggle being part of an incredible empire?

So let's take a look at the Brits who currently have Queen Elizabeth II as their monarch. There are times, I imagine, when she is presenting herself as queen in regalia and crown and a train more beautiful than that of a bride when her family need to remember her position and show honor and follow protocol like everybody else.

And there are times, I imagine, after dinner in the royal palace, when she kicks off her shoes and sits by the fireplace and snuggle with the family, and they can chat and laugh and reflect on the day. Still, there are times when a member of the family has a problem that they would like her to address, and they need to make a formal request and submit a proper petition despite the fact that she is *family.*

So too with God. One must be mindful that He is massively important and head of a tremendous empire and there are times when He is praised and honored in a formal context and commands an incredible amount of respect.

And there are times when His children might have an issue, an illness, a debt that can't be payed, and they must submit a request to Him in the form of a prayer (I feel the Holy Spirit's attention on this), yet there are other times when you feel His presence in a special way and you are sure He's just thrown His arms around you and kissed you on the forehead—in His loving role as God the Father. His attention reminds you that you are a loved member of His royal family.

Seventh, the Kingdom of God is often understated (I felt the Holy Spirit's attention on that), as I am sure it has been here because it is impossible to fathom the expansiveness and power of that incredible empire! Yet Jesus starts us on the road of discovery by making entry possible.

"Great is the Lord and most worthy of praise, his greatness no one can fathom" (Psalm 145:11, NIV).

* * * * * * *

Now each one of us has a decision to make—whether to take the opportunity to accept Jesus as Lord and receive Kingdom citizenship or continue without it. Life without the Kingdom is like life on an island struggling with poverty. It is up to each one of us to reach for more, to not settle for a life of poverty when, as Jesus reminds us, the Kingdom of God is near. (See Matthew 4:17.)

> Now to the King eternal, immortal, invisible, the only God, be honor and glory for ever and ever. Amen. (1 Timothy 1:17, NIV)

33

The Backstory

Note: the form of bullfighting discussed in this section is "bloodless" where the bull is not harmed. This author does not endorse cruelty to animals.

I was a graduate student taking a screenwriting class and my script, *Maria the Bullfighter*, was being "workshopped." My classmates and instructor were pulling it apart and critiquing it. A lot was said that day, but one statement from my instructor stands out the most. "No one is going to want to see a film about bullfighting," he said.

It's not about bullfighting. It is and it isn't. It's about a woman who enters bullfighting after a violent attack on her life in order to regain her sense of strength—in order to get over feeling broken and helpless. So it is about a woman who feels wounded trying desperately to find her footing—a failed attempt to become whole using her own methods, apart from God.

At the end of the story, after winning a fight in one of Spain's notorious bullrings, Maria realizes that the brokenness she feels is still there, and at that moment, she drives off to an isolated spot to be alone with God. As she crumbles and comes to pieces, it makes room for conversation with God—a friendship forms and a heart begins to mend. She experiences this incredible metamorphosis at the side of a mountain during a whispered prayer. She becomes born again.

The "backstory" in this script are those pieces of Maria's history that reveal motivation; bits of information that helps the viewer to see that it's not so much about bullfighting as it is about the redemption of her soul.

* * * * * * *

In screenwriting, the backstory is the history of the characters and events that bring us up to the current moment. Sometimes, pieces of the backstory will reveal itself as the story unfolds in order to help the viewer understand why the characters do what they do, what led to their decisions.

So too the Kingdom of God has backstory, pieces of history that will help us understand how earth got into its current condition and why. The backstory of the Kingdom (as it relates to Earth) will help us see the whole picture, the true motives behind current action. The Bible gives us a good summary of this from the very first page.

Let's go to the "movies," back in time to primitive Earth, to a mesmerizing Garden, and watch an incredible real-life story unfold in "three acts" and seeping with backstory. Imagine this:

Act I. Scene I. As our movie opens, God is hovering above the earth. In this scene, we see the earth is already populated. God has created birds, fish in the sea, trees, and crawly creatures. But it's missing something. Earth needs a caretaker, so God created Adam and Eve. Then God said, "Let us make mankind in our image, in our likeness, so that they may rule over the fish in the sea and the birds in the sky, over the livestock and all the wild animals, and over all the creatures that move along the ground" (Genesis 1:26, NIV).

That was God the King doing what kings do—exercising His power, creating and commanding. In a bold move, He created man in His image and commanded them to have dominion. He gave Adam authority to rule over Earth.

In other words, Earth is a "territory" in His Kingdom; it is something God created and established. Then He installed Adam over this territory as a type of governor.

Scene II. Adam steps up to rule. Adam steps into his role as governor over the earth by starting small. He would name all the animals. Naming would be a demonstration of his authority and dominion.

> Now the Lord God had formed out of the ground all the wild animals and all the birds in the sky. He brought them to the man to see what he would name them; and whatever the man called each living creature, that was its name... (Genesis 2:19–20, NIV)

Adam is off to a successful start, but God sees the whole story; and so He tells Adam and Eve, as they live a blissful life in the Garden of Eden, that they needed to be careful not to do one thing (I felt the Holy Spirit's attention on this). He told them not to eat of the tree of the knowledge of good and evil because that would only expose them to death! (See Genesis 2:17.)

Adam and Eve already knew "good," having been made by God and in His image (see Genesis 1:26), but they were yet unfamiliar with "evil." They were innocent.

So God warned Adam and Eve not to eat of the tree of the knowledge of good and evil! They had to trust Him on that because they couldn't see the whole story—that the devil, that snake in the Garden, was waiting to attach itself to their lives!

Scene III. Trouble arrives. The serpent that found its way into the Garden is an enemy of the throne of God, called satan (the devil), a power-hungry created being that led a revolt in Heaven sometime earlier. (See Isaiah 14:12–15.) God responded and, "[T]he devil... who deceives the whole world...was cast down to earth; and his angels were cast down with him" (Revelations 12:9, NKJV). Now, the devil roamed the earth with a mission to kill, steal, and destroy (see John 10:10–29), beginning with Adam and Eve.

While Adam and Eve were being schooled by God on taking authority and ruling Earth, the devil was trying to think of ways to steal that authority. The devil wanted to rule Earth and everything in it, and Adam and Eve were in the way. So he came up with a plan to weaken Adam and Eve and separate them from God. The devil wanted them to distrust God.

The devil also wanted the added benefit of stopping the Kingdom of God from dominating the earth. The plan was to stop Adam and Eve. Stop them from getting strong in the earth and stop them from taking authority and dominion. In other words, the devil wanted to derail the plan of God (see Genesis 6:5–6).

God, fully aware of the devil's menacing plan, warned Adam and Eve to stay away from anything that has to do with the devil! In short, avoid the tree of the knowledge of good and evil because that knowledge of evil is mind-blowing and would tank their God-given destiny.

Once Adam and Eve's eyes were opened to evil (once they had knowledge of evil), there would be no turning back. It would be impossible for Adam and Eve to undo the event.

Scene IV. The devil brings poison. Knowledge is "the fact or con-dition of having information or of being learned."[33] For someone to receive knowledge, they need a teacher. If Adam and Eve were to eat of the tree of the knowledge of good and evil, who would teach them evil? Who would impart that knowledge?

As the devil walked through the Garden of Eden, his objective was to get Adam and Eve under his tutelage. The devil wanted to connect his mind to their mind, to impart knowledge of evil, to teach them to be weak and fearful, and to introduce death and decline.

So it became imperative to the devil that Adam and Eve eat of the tree of the knowledge of good and evil because it would open a "portal" to the devil to introduce himself into their minds, to lead them away from God (see 2 Corinthians 11:3.) Once he had access to their minds, he would move to corrupt their minds by bombard-ing their minds with fear, violence, hate, strife, hopelessness, pornog-raphy, perversions, and every type of evil.

Once the devil had their attention, he would bully (a confused and stunned) Adam into submission, steal his authority to rule earth, and simultaneously cut short the Kingdom's full manifestation in the earth.

That was a huge deal because the Kingdom of God is a massive power source and is wealthy and world changing! Adam's alignment with the Kingdom would propel him toward a dazzling future, and Adam would be taught up by the King Himself on being an effective ruler of Earth! It was an opportunity beyond imagination! But it required Adam's obedience to God. It required allegiance and loyalty to the Kingdom!

The devil's strategy is always to work through the mind by "blinding" the mind, or shutting the person off from the truth, and injecting lies. "[T]he god of this age has blinded the minds of the unbelievers, so that they cannot see the light of the gospel…" (2 Corinthians 4:4, ESV; see also 2 Corinthians 11:3).

Act II. Scene I. The devil tricks Adam and steals his authority to rule. With Adam and Eve both present, the devil went to work in the Garden by approaching Eve first.

"Now the serpent was more crafty than any of the wild animals the Lord had made. He said to the woman, 'Did God really say, "You must not eat from any tree in the garden?"'" (Genesis 3:1, NIV).

Eve answered, "We may eat fruit from the trees in the garden, but God did say, 'You must not eat fruit from the tree that is in the middle of the garden, and you must not touch it, or you will die'" (Genesis 3:2, NIV).

The serpent then said, "You will not surely die…For God knows that when you eat from it your eyes will be opened, and you will be like God, knowing good and evil" (Genesis 3:4, NIV).

Scene II. Adam and Eve step off the "cliff." Eve reached over and picked the fruit from the tree of the knowledge of good and evil and took a bite. Then she convinced Adam to do the same, and they both ate. (See Genesis 3.)

If this were an actual movie, this might be the place where light flashes across the screen with drums beating and a whistling sound cutting through the trees! Adam and Eve are about to have their "spiritual eyes" opened to the knowledge of evil. They are about to look straight into the face of the devil!

What they saw horrified them! Their eyes were "opened" to evil, to the nature of the devil, the destroyer. They could probably feel a wave of evil in every cell of their body as they realized that the serpent standing before them wanted nothing more than to kill them and their future children (I felt God's attention on this, the heart of the Father).

The devil, the destroyer, probably hurried to terrify them in their minds with evil knowledge. They might have felt like fainting, hiding, running. They covered up their nakedness and hid among the trees of the Garden like frightened animals. (See Genesis 3:8.)

The same capacity they had to "know" God, where God could access their thought life, strengthen and build them up, was now also possible in the dark realm, where the devil could now connect with and access their thought life, discourage and tear them down by planting thoughts of fear and destruction!

The Kingdom of God was on standby with a counterplan, later to manifest in the Son of God—a redemption plan to save all of Adam's offspring and to take authority from the devil and return it to man.

* * * * * * *

Later, when Adam and Eve "heard the sound of the Lord God as he was walking in the garden in the cool of the day...they hid from the Lord God among the trees in the garden" (Genesis 3:8, NIV). Adam and Eve were showing signs of the devil's influence. They were being impacted by the kingdom of darkness.

By hiding and being occupied with fear, Adam left room for the devil to step in and rule. In effect, the devil stole authority to rule over the earth (I felt the Holy Spirit's attention on this). The devil was able to steal authority because Adam didn't object (I felt God's attention on this), but let the devil do whatever he wanted.

Even after Adam's blunder, there was a window of opportunity for Adam to push back, to resist the devil. Instead, Adam resisted God when he should have been resisting the devil. As it says in scripture: "Submit yourselves, then, to God. Resist the devil, and he will flee from you" (James 4:7, NIV). So Adam failed by submitting to the devil and resisting God.

From that time forward, instead of the love of God (the Kingdom of God) wholly influencing Adam and Eve, the devil gained at least partial yet significant influence and began to impose himself on humanity as ruler over the earth.

The devil's perverted reign and rule is referred to as the "kingdom of darkness," and he is referred to as the ruler of demons (see Matthew 9:34 and 12:24). In another place, the devil is referred to as the ruler of this world (see John 14:30) with a goal of destruction (see John 10:10–29)!

* * * * * * *

God had warned Adam and Eve that they would die if they ate of the fruit of the tree of knowledge of good and evil—meaning death, the demonic and perverting spirit of satan, would infiltrate their thoughts and build a culture of darkness in their minds to eventually "distort" their identity and destroy them, cutting their lives short!

The devil "was a murderer from the beginning, not holding to the truth, for there is no truth in him. When he lies, he speaks his native language, for he is a liar and the father of lies" (John 8:44, NIV).

Until the devil's infiltration, God had substantial, if not exclusive influence in their minds; in which case, Adam and Eve were on track for a Garden of Eden lifestyle, without worry. The Garden of Eden had a peace culture, Heaven on earth. When they ate of the tree of the knowledge of good and evil, with the trickery of the devil, their thinking was corrupted, and they stepped into a fear culture.

As a result, they could no longer live in the Garden of Eden. They were evicted to keep them from making matters worse.

Act III. Scene I. A massive plan of redemption. God counterpunches by rolling out a radical and innovative idea! He will send Jesus—His only Son (I feel the Holy Spirit's attention on this)—to pay the penalty for Adam and Eve's sins (and the rest of humanity) and take back authority from the devil!

There might have been drama in the heavens when the Son of God came on the scene—perhaps a thunderbolt, the kind that sends chills through a person's soul. Some two thousand years ago, Heaven watched with massive anticipation as the Son of God descended to earth.

Jesus came to earth with a radical mission: to "destroy the devil's work" (1 John 3:8, NIV) and to reconnect people to the Kingdom of God (see Colossians 1:13). Stepping into the scene as the "last Adam," Jesus is God's incredibly courageous solution to man's fall.

* * * * * * *

Adam sinned when he disobeyed God in the Garden and continued to sin when he abandoned his authority to rule Earth and lived in fear. The rest of mankind would inherit that sin nature and continue to decline.

The penalty of sin is death, and Jesus arrives on Earth to pay that penalty for all of humanity (see Romans 6:23). It was not an easy price to pay and involved scourging, humiliation, death on a cross, and descending into hell for three days and three nights! (See Matthew 12:40.) But then, in a show of immense power and strength, He rises from the grave, triumphing over death—demonstrating that death has no power over Him! (See 1 Corinthians 15:3–4.)

His death and resurrection demonstrate His authority in the earth. In other words, He took authority back from the devil—the authority the devil stole from Adam.

When Jesus saw His disciples after the resurrection from the dead, He told them that He had accomplished His mission. "...All authority in heaven and on earth has been given to me" (Matthew 28:18, NIV). He then gave authority back to mankind. He told His followers, "I have given you authority...to overcome all the power of the enemy; nothing will harm you" (Luke 10:19, NIV).

* * * * * * *

The relationship God has wanted from the beginning is now possible; but that relationship can only be established through the born-again experience, by accepting Jesus the Christ (I felt the Holy Spirit's attention on this) as Lord and Savior, by becoming a "follower" of Jesus. In scripture, Jesus says, "I am the way and the truth and the life. No one comes to the Father except through me" (John 14:6, NIV). Now, "For the believer there is hope beyond the grave, because Jesus Christ has opened the door to heaven for us by His death and resurrection" (Billy Graham).[34] (See also Romans 5:10–11).

The new birth closes the gap the devil created with his lies. It is a tremendous opportunity to realign with the Kingdom of God and cut the devil's efforts short. (I see the devil's attention on this.) That's the one thing the devil hopes you never realize—the enormous power and benefit of the new birth experience and how incredibly powerful and effective it is in releasing you from his grip! The new birth brings you out of darkness and *into* the Kingdom!

So in an incredible act of love, Jesus frees us from death, from the power of sin, from the devil's kingdom of darkness, and restores proper relationship with God (see Romans 6:15–23, 3:21–24).

In other words, the Kingdom of God is back! (I felt the Holy Spirit's attention on this). Back to the forefront, and Jesus makes entry possible!

Scene II. In the end, God is not satisfied with simply rescuing humanity. He plans to demolish the kingdom of darkness. As the Kingdom of God readies itself to destroy the kingdom of darkness, Jesus sends out a call to every soul to take shelter under the shadow of His "wings," to get out the way!

Jesus, with hands stretched out and eyes that urge every person to accept His invitation, sees the end of the story. He knows the whole picture, and what He sees causes Him to weep in compassion for humanity. He sees a people not taking this thing seriously.

> For the wages of sin is death, but the gift
> of God is eternal life in Christ Jesus our Lord.
> (Romans 6:23, NIV)

Those who pass up the opportunity for salvation in Jesus Christ are on their own, left to manage the consequences of their sins and separation from God.

God, in extreme acts of mercy, sent Jesus to perform the rescue, and so it is that the Bible promises: "If you declare with your mouth, 'Jesus is Lord,' and believe in your heart that God raised him from the dead, you will be saved" (Romans 10:9, NIV).

"As scripture says, 'Anyone who believes in him will never be put to shame'" (Romans 10:11, NIV). Jesus said, "Whoever comes to me I will never drive away" (John 6:37, NIV).

The devil will surely attach to the lives of anyone who is not "covered" by the blood of Jesus. "This is how it will be at the end of the age. The angels will come and separate the wicked from the righteous and throw them into the blazing furnace, where there will be weeping and gnashing of teeth" (Matthew 13:49, NIV).

Scene III. "In development." How the rest of the story plays out will depend on each one of us, the choices we make. Each individual now has a "Garden of Eden" moment where one must choose to submit to God and His Kingdom, to receive salvation through Jesus Christ or, by default, to submit to the devil and his doomed kingdom of darkness.

God has provided a radical and effective answer by sending His Son. He is saying, "Choose life so that you and your children may live." (See Deuteronomy 30:15–20.)

"God so loved the world that he gave his one and only Son, that whoever believes in him shall not perish but have eternal life" (John 3:16, NIV). He is opportunity at the door. To receive Jesus as Lord and Savior, say this simple prayer:

Prayer of Salvation

"Dear Lord Jesus, I know I am a sinner, and I ask for your forgiveness. I believe you died for my sins and rose from the dead. I trust and follow you as my Lord and Savior. Guide my life and help me to do your will. In your name, amen."[35]

Once you accept Jesus as Lord, He will send you a Comforter—The Holy Spirit, who will stay with you and help you through the process of salvation and will be with you forever. (See John 14:16; see also Acts 2:1–5.) With the Holy Spirit by your side, you will never have to face life alone!

* * * * * *

God knows all the details of our backstory and lovingly reaches for us, offering healing, inclusion, forgiveness, and a future and a hope. (See Jeremiah 29:11). All of that becomes possible when we align ourselves with His Kingdom!

Kingdom alignment is an incredible benefit of salvation!

Kingdom Privileges
and Duties

34

Kingdom Privileges and Duties

As the woman stepped through the church doors, she clung to the hope that God would heal her crippled daughter. How she must have wished that her daughter could walk and run and play like other children. But after the pastor prayed for the sick, her daughter seemed just as crippled as before.

Then later as the woman was bathing her child in a bathtub, she heard a cracking sound. She looked down and saw the child's legs being snapped into place (I felt God's attention on this) and realigned (I felt the Holy Spirit's attention on this). The little girl's legs were perfectly restored!

This true story about an incredible creative miracle demonstrates the power of the Kingdom of God in transforming lives! Healing is one of the many privileges of the Kingdom!

* * * * * * *

Every kingdom offers some basic privileges to its citizens. Let's take another look at the United Kingdom (UK), for example.

Citizens of the UK gain certain benefits by the mere fact that they were born into that kingdom. They have free national health coverage,[36] are free to seek employment in the region without a work permit,[37] and they can travel in the region without a visa, including anywhere in the European Union (EU) and Switzerland. [38]

So, too, the Kingdom of God provides certain benefits to every citizen, including health services, employment opportunities, and even travel benefits.

In the area of health benefits, your citizenship gets you eternal life. "[T]he free gift of God is eternal life in Christ Jesus our Lord" (Romans 6:23, see also John 3:16). Living forever is the ultimate health benefit! So as a Kingdom-citizen, you get a spiritual "body" that allows you to function in this present life, as well as exist in God's Kingdom, forever.

Fortunately, you don't have to wait until you get to Heaven to be well. While on Earth, Kingdom citizens have special access to healing. So if your earthly body gets ill, God has an answer. As scripture says, by the stripes of Jesus you are healed. (See Isaiah 53:5.) You have a Kingdom health insurance plan that Jesus purchased on the cross; but you have to realize that it is there and learn how to access it.

Employment opportunities also belong to each person born into the Kingdom, since we are all "employed" to spread the gospel of Jesus, the Christ. "He said to them, 'Go into all the world and preach the gospel to all creation'" (Mark 16:15). That is the mandate for every born-again believer—to tell people that Jesus saves! We all share the responsibility (I felt God's attention on this) of sharing the gospel no matter our "earthly" occupation. And our work will be compensated. Jesus says, "...Behold, I am coming quickly, and My reward is with Me, to give to everyone according to his work" (Revelations 22:12, NIV).

You even have the benefits of travel. That may be in the performance of Kingdom duties, such as travelling to another country as a missionary or evangelist. Sometimes it is to the heavenly realm, for whatever reason—discovery, healing, or peace—you get the privilege of getting there without a visa!

But Kingdom living is not just about blessings and receiving from God. Each citizen has responsibilities; there are expectations of how we are to conduct ourselves and contribute to the Household of God. For example, we are expected to repent from sins (1 John 3:9), help each other (Galatians 6:2), partner with God in bringing order (1 Corinthians 3:9–11), respect and honor God (1 Peter 2:17), and be loyal to the throne (Psalm 78:8).

35

Kingdom Privilege

Citizenship

Now, therefore you are no longer strangers and foreigners, but
fellow citizens of the saints and members of the household of God.
—Ephesians 2:19 (NKJV)

One winter day while reclining on a couch in front of a fireplace and enjoying the warmth from the fire, I began to doze off; and in that mysterious place between sleep and wake, I had an amazing vision! I was still aware of the room, the fire in the fireplace, and the couch; but for a split second, my spiritual eyes were opened, and I saw my "born-again" spirit! I was startled to see that I was made of pure white light from head to toe. My hair, my hands, even my clothes glowed as a laid there as a body of white light.

At that moment, I knew that I was seeing my newborn spirit in Christ Jesus. I was observing the resultant regenerative power of God the Holy Spirit. Children of God are made in His image, and He is pure light.

As it says in scripture, "This is the message we have heard from him and declare to you: God is light, in him there is no darkness at all" (1 John 1:5, NIV).

* * * * * * *

So how does a person born of earthly parents become a child of the Light? When one accepts Jesus as Lord, a new birth occurs. That person transitions from death to life and from darkness to light. (See Colossians 1:12–14.)

We are saved "through the washing of regeneration and renewing of the Holy Spirit" (Titus 3:5). That means you are literally regenerated, renewed—in other words, born again, but not in the flesh, in spirit. The old spirit is extinguished, and a new spirit is born.

So once I accepted Jesus as Lord, Jesus immediately went to work taking my sins upon Himself and paying the penalty on the cross. The Holy Spirit takes it from there, and He "extinguished" my old spirit and "formed" a new spirit in me. As one author explained, "To be born again is to experience a second genesis. It is a new beginning; a fresh start in life…regeneration by the Holy Spirit is a… radical change into a new kind of being."[39]

* * * * * * *

The new birth is into something and into someplace; you are born into the family of God and into His Kingdom.

Just as in the natural, you become a citizen of wherever you are born, so too in the Kingdom of God. The New Birth brings Kingdom citizenship. As it says in scripture, "But our citizenship is in heaven. And we eagerly await a Savior from there, the Lord Jesus Christ" (Philippians 3:20, NIV). (See also 1 Peter 1:3.) "God raised us from death to life with Christ Jesus, and he has given us a place beside Christ in heaven" (Ephesians 2:6, NIV).

So a shift occurs when a person is born again. They are spiritually "delivered" from the power of the devil, and they spiritually "transition" into Kingdom citizenship.

> [A]nd giving joyful thanks to the Father, who has qualified you to share in the inheritance of his holy people in the kingdom of light. For he has rescued us from the dominion of darkness and brought us into the kingdom of the son he loves, in whom we have redemption, the forgiveness of sins. (Colossians 1:12–14, NIV)

The work of the Holy Spirit is to continue to carry out the redemption of mankind through these rebirths. In other words, redemption involves bringing souls into the Kingdom of God through a new birth.[40] Entering the Kingdom of God *requires* a born-again experience (I felt the Holy Spirit's attention on this) by accepting Jesus as Lord. In scripture, "Jesus declared, 'I tell you the truth, no one can see the kingdom of God unless they are born again'" (John 3:3, NIV)

With the new birth, the devil's reign ends, and the reign of God begins in the individual's life. The devil's kingdom of darkness loses dominion, authority, and power to rule the individual's life, and God gains dominion, authority, and power to rule. The Kingdom of God becomes the ruling force in that individual's life and future!

* * * * * * *

The transition from darkness means deliverance from the power of sin, from death and disease, from poverty, from all the powers of the devil and his demons. (See Luke 10:19.)

It also means transitioning into a magnificent Kingdom of power, wealth, wisdom, and technology beyond our imagination! (I felt the Holy Spirit's attention on this.)

If you have accepted Jesus as Lord and Savior, you are forgiven of all your sins. The old you passed away, and you are made new in Christ Jesus! The old sins and pitfalls no longer have any place in your life.

Through the new birth, we are born in the *likeness* of God through the creative and regenerative power of the Holy Spirit; and our new "form" allows us to exist in God's realm, come under God's authority, and function in His Kingdom. Those born of God immediately begin life in a theocracy.[41]

The born-again believer can claim this verse of scripture:

> But you are a chosen people, a royal priesthood, a holy nation, God's special possession, that you may declare the praises of him who called you out of darkness into his wonderful light. Once you were not a people, but now you are the people of God; once you had not received mercy, but now you have received mercy. (1 Peter 2:9–10, NIV)

That mercy is enormous! It includes the opportunity to exist in the Kingdom of God with the gift of eternal life—a great future as citizens of the Kingdom—under the authority of God.

36

Kingdom Privilege

Healing

S andra's heart must have been pounding as the doctor gave her the diagnosis! She must have heard the stories of people dying horrific and painful deaths from the disease; now it was at her door.

She told me the story as I stood in line waiting for the sanctuary doors to open at a church conference in New York City. Those standing around me listened as well, nearly leaning in as the animated black woman with short kinky hair spoke as quickly as she could form the sentences.

When Sandra got the HIV/AIDS diagnosis, the doctors had no cure for the disease and gave her very little hope, so she had to look outside medical science for a solution. She must have heard the Bible stories: the woman healed of an issue of blood (see Luke 8:43–48) and the blind man who received his sight by the merciful acts of the Messiah (see Matthew 20:33). She found hope. (I felt God's attention on that.)

She turned to Jesus and invited Him into her heart, that same heart where the killer virus was running rampant, and she prayed for complete deliverance.

Meanwhile, Sandra's doctors had set a series of appointments for her to discuss her diagnosis and address chances of survival and whatever limited remedies they had to prolong her life.

One day, she went to her appointment while clinging to the prayer that God would heal her. When she got to the doctor's office, she was instructed to go to a nearby room where the doctor would be waiting to discuss her case.

When Sandra entered the room, she was startled by what she saw: the room was filled with doctors lining the walls, standing at attention with clipboards in their hands. Apparently, the clipboards had her diagnosis as well as the most recent results.

One of the doctors spoke up and revealed the reason for the crowd. He said, "Sandra, we don't understand it, but there is no more sign of HIV/AIDS in your blood. Matter of fact, your blood is like a newborn baby's."

At that point, Sandra lost control and a prayer in tongues[42] gushed from her soul as she celebrated God's goodness and gave Him thanks!

As she stood there praying and thanking Jesus, the team of baffled doctors looked on in amazement! *How is this possible?* They seemed to be wondering how Someone managed to defy their diagnosis! *Who does that?* Someone had stepped into Sandra's life and changed their scientific results.

Now, an avid follower of Jesus—the Someone that had won her heart and, by the power of the Holy Spirit, cleared her life of the disease, inspires her to tell anyone who will listen—salvation in Jesus includes total deliverance!

* * * * * * *

"God anointed Jesus of Nazareth with the Holy Spirit and power, and...he went around doing good and healing all who were under the power of the devil because God was with him" (Acts 10:38, NIV). When Jesus was surrounded by large crowds, He "was moved with compassion for them and healed their sick" (Matthew 14:4,

NKJV). In fact, "great multitudes followed Him and He healed them all" (Matthew 12:15, NKJV).

* * * * * *

God hasn't changed. His desire is still to see His citizens living free from the effects of sin and illness. The first step is to accept Jesus as Lord. The second crucial step (I feel the Holy Spirit's attention on this) is to seek the Kingdom of God, above all else.

It makes sense that as we align our lives with the Kingdom of God and live a lifestyle that is aligned with the commands of God, that a more victorious life will take form.

Living a Kingdom lifestyle is a process that requires patience, prayer, and study. As a child of God, and a citizen of Heaven, all that you need is found in His Kingdom, and that includes healing.

Sandra was healed because she tapped into one of her privileges as a citizen of Heaven; she repented of her sins and trusted God for healing, and that Kingdom access saved her life!

37

Kingdom Privilege

Employment

My grandmother used to cry when she told the story. One Jamaican day her young son, Lenny, came to her and told her that he was hungry, and it was his voice with all the other voices that made her lash out. She told him to go away. Shortly after, she found him dead, with worms coming from his mouth. He starved to death, and agony, the testimony of his sorrowful life, flowed from him, twisted and miserable. So for a time in my life, I wanted to be a doctor. I wanted to be whatever I needed to be to end the bad stories that leaked from my family's history.

I wanted to make a difference. So when I was able to come to the United States many years later, as I sat in my car by a sunny harbor, with a lighthouse behind me and a majestic sea in front of me, I asked God, "What do you want me to be?" What is my purpose; what is my calling?

I was waiting, as I watched the blue sea shimmy in sunlight, for Him to say, "Doctor." But He said, "Writer." Writer? Writer!? It was the one thing I *didn't* want to be. I knew it would mean spending too much time in my head, too much time inside on sunny days tapping away on a keyboard, and too much time alone; but I didn't know that it would mean that I would find Him, His sweet calm Voice in the pages of story, in those lonely secret gardens of my heart. I found Him in that quiet place. He met me on page 86, spoke kindness to me on page 17 and on and on it went, until I fell into His arms in conclusion.

* * * * * *

I am a citizen of the Kingdom of God, and my employment, from the lips of the Father, is writing, and I am so glad that I said "yes" to His call.

I am learning that I will always find Him in the pages of purpose.

Kingdom citizen, what is *your* calling? Find it and you will find Him.

Share your vision, find encouragement at Faithbridgecafe.com.

38

Kingdom Privilege

Wisdom and Direction

I was on the interstate, stuck in traffic, looking at the tail end of cars in front of me, when suddenly, my face went numb! It felt like I had shots of Novocain that crawled up from my lips to my cheek and nose. As I sat in the long line of strangers, all of us rushing home after a long day of work in the city, I felt a sickening feeling come over me. *What is this? Am I having a stroke?* I tried to move my lips and wiggle my nose, hoping it was just an allergy, maybe reaction to pollen, or perhaps a pinched nerve.

I checked for signs of a stroke. My speech was fine, no drooping on one side of my face, no weakness on one side of my body, just the numbness.

I felt well enough to drive, so I went directly home, went to my computer and began to do some research. *Am I over-reacting? Is there a logical explanation for all this?* Words like diabetes, multiple sclerosis, a pinched nerve, peripheral neuropathy, and severe food allergies, flashed across my computer screen.

The next morning, when I woke and tried to stand, I noticed that my head and upper back were throbbing, as if the nerves were firing off in all directions. I felt week and wobbly and barely made it to the bathroom. I thought back to my decisions over the past few months. I ate fairly good meals, but looking back, I could see I had some bad habits.

Along with a watermelon binging and tuna habit, I craved sweets (I felt the Holy Spirit's attention on this) and had cookies and muffins whenever I visited my favorite health food store.

I felt toxic.

As I sat alone in my room and prayed, I had a vision of a balance scale, and one side was lower than the other. I knew it meant that my life was off balance, but more importantly, I took it as a cue that if I could regain balance, I would see improvement. I started to examine my life the way an architect examines a bridge for cracks—with a good amount of urgency.

My mind drifted back to more than a year ago when I received a word from God to lay off the sweets. I did for some time, but like the slight of a magician's hand, it crept back into my life, first as a treat once in a while, then as a daily routine.

I was also commuting four hours a day, two hours each way, and often working an eight-hour shift, giving me a whopping twelve-hour day from start to finish. The commute was *not* relaxing. It was maniac, with back to back traffic for nearly the entire two hours. I'd arrive to work tired. I was only getting about five or six hours of sleep at night and crashing in exhaustion on weekends.

I took this job in the city as a temporary assignment that was meant to last six weeks, determining that I could manage it short-term (I felt God's attention on this). Four months later, it was still on my plate. The company liked me so much that they were talking about creating a regional role, all along the East Coast, where I would travel and manage staffing needs at various locations. I was tempted. I imagined a good salary and a good amount of independence.

Meanwhile, I had my writing ministry on standby (I felt the Holy Spirit's attention on this), barely having time to write; but I kept thinking that I would leave the job after another week. But the weeks rolled on, and several months later, I was still pushing myself to keep going.

The biggest challenge for me in "full-time" ministry is waiting for the payoff, writing for months and years at a time with no substantial income. I didn't mind getting a "regular" job and working hard, I just hated to struggle as a writer. I had a roof over my head and enough to eat, but I wasn't living the life I wanted.

So I was working non-stop because financial independence provided a sense of accomplishment. I had a vision of buying my own house instead of living with relatives, getting a different car, one that didn't have over two hundred thousand miles and leaks everywhere; and it felt good to be able to go into the market and pick up whatever I wanted. However. I never meant for my health to swing out of control.

I was aware too that I was being pulled away from ministry, and I felt tired and overwhelmed and kept promising myself I'd make a change, that I'd go back to writing once I saved up a few more paychecks.

At some point a shift occurred. (I felt the Holy Spirit's attention on this.) My days were fully occupied with work and grabbing a bit of sleep before going back to work. I got so busy that I had little time to think of how it was affecting my life on a deeper level; how it was affecting my true calling, my ministry. It was almost as if I was on autopilot, and each tiring, unhealthy day, blended into the next, until I looked up and months had passed by.

As I sat in highway traffic each morning and evening, trying to manage a mountain of exhaustion, I knew my days were too frantic! I'd say to God, "I need my life back," but yet, I kept pushing, thinking that if I could just get a certain amount saved up, then I would cut back on the craziness.

For the past few months, I felt God telling me to pull back, to ease up on my schedule, to rest. I didn't ignore Him, but I was slow to comply, thinking of it often, but never getting around to making the change.

Then one evening, I felt God tell me that He was going to intervene. I had a vision of Him reaching down from Heaven and pulling me from a situation. I suspected that it was related to work.

Shortly after that vision, I was sitting in traffic, checking the numbness in my face, and fighting back the panic.

That incident forced my hand. Do I continue to push through this crazy schedule to keep that paycheck, to keep saving for that house, to get a different car? Do I even have a choice at this point; why is my face numb? I did some quick prioritizing and repenting, followed by several hours of damage assessment. (I felt God's attention on that.)

* * * * * * *

After a few more symptoms developed the following day, I headed for the emergency room. After tests, including blood tests, urine tests, and a way too quick visit from the emergency room physician, I had the results: all my tests came back normal. Besides low blood pressure, they couldn't find anything wrong. The doctor explained that the ER was limited and beyond testing my vitals and running a few routine exams, the rest was for my primary care physician. He finished talking while he exited the room, his sentences trailing off as he walked away, leaving me sitting there, my heart filled with questions.

With a visit to the primary care physician sometime in the future, I had time to think. I needed to find my footing, so I went for a drive by the sea.

* * * * * * *

I found a little beachy town covered in a sweet mist and cool breeze, and I walked. I didn't know where the streets would lead, but I headed toward the water, and kept along the coast, feeling the damp air and watching the water appear between houses, then disappear behind their walls, then re-appear again.

It was quiet; no one walking except me, no cars driving by, no one on their porches, just me, bursts of flowers in gardens by the side of the road, and the quick wings of small birds as they scurry over the roof tops.

And I prayed and breathed in salty air. When it started to rain, the drops tapping the rim of my summer hat, I exhaled and inhaled.

As I drove away from Woods Hole, my mind calm and a piano melody filling the air around me, I could go again; I could go to the place I left with the room filled with questions, and I could unpack them one at a time and reach for God.

* * * * * * *

I started with sugar. I cut out the watermelon binges, starches, and sweets. I had a nagging suspicion that I might be diabetic or pre-diabetic. I knew it was important to avoid all sweets. (I felt the Holy Spirit's attention on that.)

In the next breath, I was cutting back on my schedule. I sent an email to management requesting to drop back to two days a week instead of the usual five days. I felt the re-assuring presence of God at that moment, as if we were finally in agreement.

To follow up on my theory of diabetes or pre-diabetes, I picked up a blood glucose kit at the pharmacy. When I finally got the courage to prick my finger for a blood sample, I found that indeed, my blood sugar level was about thirty-five points too high. At least now some of the symptoms made sense. I immediately boosted my eating habits, adding greens, more fiber, protein and water.

I continued to pray to God for guidance and was attentive to any cues on improving my health. I leaned on His word that promises, "If any of you lacks wisdom, you should ask of God, who gives generously to all without finding fault, and it will be given to you" (James 15, NIV).

I started to receive wisdom through visions. For example, I had an open vision of tamarind[43], Tuscan kale,[44] and beef liver. Intrigued, I did some research online and found that some experiments show tamarind is effective in managing blood sugar levels, while Tuscan kale adds fiber and antioxidants, and helps with detoxing. Liver[45] is packed with nutrients.

In ten days of paying attention to God and asking for wisdom, listening when He "speaks," resting, changing my work schedule, eating a more balanced diet, eliminating added sugars, and adding organic kale and tamarind, organic beef liver, plus vitamin supplements, my blood glucose level dropped within normal range and I began to feel better.

I made a commitment to myself to keep going with this lifestyle change and was pleased to see that I dropped five pounds of body fat, bringing me within a healthy weight for my height.

* * * * * * *

Oftentimes, the pieces that lead to illness are multi-layered; but the idea, I understand, is to change what can be changed and leave the rest to God. (I felt the Holy Spirit's attention on that.)

We move forward now, God and I, on a different road than the one I used to "travel." He doesn't have to say anything; I can sense His commitment to my health and well-being, to my full recovery. I have His word, and I am grateful for His patience.

I am also sure of this: as disturbing as that facial numbness was for me, I get the feeling that incident saved me from something much worse (I felt God's attention on that, and I felt the Holy Spirit's attention on that); meaning, I had no idea my blood glucose was so high. That alert put me to work on finally making some needed changes.

In the process, I found out that I was pre-diabetic, and not full-blown diabetic, which would have presented a whole other level of challenges for me. So there is reason to be grateful. I thank God.

My goal is to live smarter, and to be careful to not get so busy that I allow "health-leaks"—those imbalances that weave themselves into a busy schedule—the ones that lead to the door of sickness.

And yes. I started exercising. Not only will I recover, but my confession is that I will recover stronger than ever before (I felt the Holy Spirit's attention on this).

The most incredible gift I got from this health crisis was seeing God at work. He intervened! He saw me struggling, drowning in my choices, and He stepped in.

God didn't orchestrate the illness I experienced, that's not His character. He did *use* it however, to pull me out a train-wrecking lifestyle of sugar-holic, workaholic habits that could have ended badly. He reached down from Heaven and pulled me out of a stressful work schedule, bad daily commute, and poor eating habits. He used the health crisis to lead me to better choices.

The health crisis got my attention, caused me to get off the work treadmill, and listen to God.

Perhaps my story will help someone who reads this book to listen sooner than I did, to heed those early warnings.

* * * * * * *

Sometimes people with the best intentions make bad choices (I felt the Holy Spirit's attention on this); but fortunate for us, God is invested in every citizen of His Kingdom, and we can go to him for wisdom in recovery.

In a crisis, God provides valuable wisdom on how to proceed. Sometimes it might be the vision of a balance scale with one side higher than the other, to tell you that your life is out of balance; or it might simply be a word to "stay calm," combined with His reassuring presence.

In a health storm, that guidance and caring attention from God is priceless. It is a Kingdom privilege—one He makes available to all His citizens.

I thank God for being invested, for helping me (I felt the Holy Spirit on that) to re-focus on what matters.

Scripture reminds us to be strong and courageous. God will never leave us or forsake us (see Deuteronomy 31:6); and when we get it wrong, He doesn't beat us down. He comes alongside and tries to correct the imbalances. He restores balance, and with a Father's heart.

Update: At the end of two weeks, I feel like myself again. That has huge value (I felt the Holy Spirit's attention on that). To feel strength, stamina, mobility, and the energy to fulfill my calling is enormous! I am a healthier version of myself. (I felt God's attention on that.) Thank God!

* * * * * * *

I'm glad the daily commute is out the way. I work two days a week now, with a day in between those two days to rest and recover, and I am back to writing. My diet is back on track and so is my ministry. I see this health challenge as an opportunity to turn my life around. (I felt the Holy Spirit on that.)

I don't have the money, don't know how I'll get that car I've wanted (I felt the Holy Spirit's attention on that), but I know God will take care of me. In any case, I am not trading my health for cash, and not trading my ministry for a new car.

The lust of money is sneaky. It can overtake someone with eyes wide open; but it won't take you out of the game so long as you abide in God, and with a sincere heart, seek first the Kingdom of God (I felt the Holy Spirit's attention on that).

Dear reader, don't be blindsided by illness. Heed God's warnings and be around for the great life and purpose He has designed for you. (I felt the Holy Spirit's attention on this.)

Are you in the process of recovering, with the help of God, from bad choices or illness? Remember, God cares about you, and as you reach for Him, He will help you by giving you peace and strategies for recovery.

Stuck in the daily grind, feeling like you need to do more and work harder, and push through your body's sign of exhaustion in order to get more stuff? There's a better way. "[S]eek first the kingdom of God and His righteousness, and all these things shall be added to you" (Matthew 6:33, NKJV).

* * * * * * *

Join the conversation at Faithbridgecafe.com.

39

Kingdom Privilege

Danger Alerts

Dark ocean. A small boat caught up in a strong wave, struggling to stay upright. Men below deck, sitting helplessly as the storm rages outside!

Above deck, a tired and frightened captain, drenched in seawater, is working desperately at the wheel to turn the boat in the direction of a towering wave rushing toward him! He is meeting the wave head on to ride over the crest of the wave before it gets too high and crushes him!

The sound of metal squeaking and the boat groaning fills the air as the little vessel clings to the base of the wave and begins to climb and climb until midway up, the captain watching as—

The wave, now several stories high, falls forward and swallows up the tiny vessel, pulling it deep into cold waters.

In the cabin below, the crew push against the cabin door, trying to escape the sinking vessel, but it's too late. A bed of water is pressing against the door on the other side! They know there is nowhere to go from here. The boat is sinking in the middle of the Atlantic; the cabin door is submerged in tons of water, and there is no one in sight.

As water seeps into the cabin, the crew seem to be making peace with death. They watch the water rise to their waist, to their shoulders, and dampen their lips. As they take their last breath, they understand that the decision they made just hours earlier led them to a grave in the belly of the ocean.

That decision was to ride into a perfect storm, totally underestimating the trouble that was ahead of them.

* * * * * * *

The movie, *The Perfect Storm* was filmed in the vibrant and sunny seacoast town of Gloucester, Massachusetts. As the movie goes, the Andrea Gail was a swordfishing boat that disappeared at sea in 1991 after getting trapped by two aggressive weather fronts: a nor'easter and a hurricane. The fishing vessel and crew were locked in by a perfect storm!

According to the movie of the real-life event, the crew was warned that storms were brewing around them, but they didn't heed the warnings. They were tempted by the amount of money they could make if they ventured out to the Flemish Cap, where the captain was certain, would be teeming with fish for a big market sale.

After a big catch, the ice machine breaks, and the crew must decide whether to risk venturing through the storm in order to preserve their catch; or wait out the storm and possibly lose their bounty, and their livelihood. The captain was convincing. They decide to go for it and rode into the storm!

It wasn't long before the boat was being pounded by massive waves, several stories high, and winds up to 90 mph. The little fishing boat struggled to stay upright. After one mammoth wave capsized the boat, the vessel managed to right itself, to the cheers of an exhausted crew, only to be pounded again with another towering wave. There is a great moment in the movie when the captain, seeing the high waves racing toward the boat, admits, "She's not going to let us out." Sadly, the crew was never seen again.

* * * * * * *

How many of us have found ourselves in a type of perfect storm, when it seems as if the trouble raging around us had no intention of letting us out? There is this great sense of exhilaration when one *does* come out on the other side.

That's how I felt when, by the grace of God, I escaped nearly being kidnapped while I was a missionary in Japan. My life was a prize to me! Were it not for God, that could have easily gone the other way; I could have been one among many missing women traveling alone in a foreign country. But I trusted God, and He showed up when I needed Him and showed me how to escape. In effect, my alignment with His Kingdom provided a door out of danger. (He came to the rescue of one of His citizens!)

At some point in life, we all seem to end up in trouble that is much bigger than us. Sometimes it's our own doing. I ended up in the car in Japan because I took a ride to a hotel from strangers. I walked into a trap. It was fortunate for me that God was with me (I felt the Holy Spirit's attention on this).

But what happens when we venture out alone, in our own strength, with motives of making money, of being famous, of meeting someone and getting married, etc., and God is not part of the equation? What do we do when a perfect storm sets in?

There is hope (I feel Jesus's attention on this)! Salvation in Jesus and *listening* to the voice of God is the answer that can push back the calamity.

In the movie, the crew of the Andrea Gail received a radio warning that there was a raging storm ahead, but they ignored the warnings and sailed into trouble; their eyes focused, perhaps, on the amount of money they would gain if they took a great risk. Unfortunately, they underestimated the storm ahead.

* * * * * * *

Are we underestimating the storm called "sin" that has gripped the planet? Earth is like the Andrea Gail and every person makes up the crew. God is speaking on the "shortwave radio" and warning us to turn back! Get out of those sinful lifestyles, return to prayer, seek His face while there is still time! Now, all of us are faced with a decision. Do we heed the voice of God, or do we push forward into deeper storm fronts, deeper levels of sin?

Are we too busy with the pursuit of wealth and self-indulgence to pay attention to His voice? Meanwhile, Earth is trapped by two aggressive weather fronts: a nor'easter and a hurricane of sinful lifestyles.

God loves the world, and so He's trying really hard to get our attention! He is calling to all humanity to turn from sin since sin leads to death. Many have not been listening (I feel the Holy Spirit's attention on this) because they don't realize the magnitude of the problem, underestimating the times ahead. Sin is pulling Earth apart! But Jesus is the answer (I feel the Holy Spirit's attention on this)!

God wants to help us all to avoid or survive life's storms, but He needs basic cooperation, such as listening to Him when He speaks and *doing* what he says! (I felt the Holy Spirit's attention on this.) He is telling everyone who will listen to repent, turn from sin, and take shelter in Jesus!

And with the help of God, with salvation in Jesus, it becomes possible to get out of those perfect storms. There is no storm too big for God to handle (I felt the Holy Spirit's attention on this). God will help anyone who calls to him to turn from sin; you don't have to go it alone. He has already provided the remedy of salvation through His Son, Jesus, the Christ. And all have sinned and fallen short of the glory of God. Every person on earth needs salvation!

Once you accept Jesus as Lord, an entire new world opens up for you. Amazingly, you not only escape death, you also receive eternal life. You enter the Kingdom of God.

This journey begins with a simple prayer. If you haven't accepted Jesus as Lord, here is a precious opportunity!

Prayer of Salvation

"Dear Lord Jesus, I know I am a sinner, and I ask for your forgiveness. I believe you died for my sins and rose from the dead. I trust and follow you as my Lord and Savior. Guide my life and help me to do your will. In your name, amen."[46]

40

Kingdom Privilege

Spiritual Support

If I were to write a screenplay about the life of King David,[47] I might choose to open the scene with David seated on a tree stump in the forest. Suddenly, he hears a whistling sound. He stands, looks around, and over there to the right, he sees his good friend, Jonathan. He smiles and walks over and embraces his friend.

We know the backstory. David is in the middle of a "storm." Jonathan's father, King Saul, has been hunting David to kill him because he is jealous of David. He knows that David is destined to replace him as King of Israel. (See 1 Samuel 16.)

Jonathan, the one who has been trying to protect David, is a true friend in a storm.

As the story progresses, we see that the "storm" is never able to defeat David. Instead, God uses the storm, the pressure, to prepare him to be king!

* * * * * *

When I realized there was a smear campaign against me, my heart sank. Why would someone do such a thing, and what exactly is being said anyway? So, I took it to God in prayer. Did you see this

245

Lord? What is going on? The Lord opened my understanding in a vision so that I clearly understood the campaign! I felt sickened by what I saw!

So, I started my own campaign—a prayer campaign! "Please show me how to fight this thing, Lord," I prayed (I felt the Holy Spirit's attention on that).

My future was being challenged! I was entering a perfect storm. Then, in the quiet, as I stood in the eye of the storm, watching the winds whirl around me, I closed my eyes and reached for the hand of God, and there, in the silence, I "heard" the soft whisper of His voice. His presence surrounded me, and I received two visions and a promise!

The first vision was of an elephant pushing against a wall. The wall seems to be by itself; but as the elephant pushed against the wall, a second wall appeared in the vision, coming in from the East, to support the first wall.

The elephant seems oblivious to the fact that the first wall now had support and just kept pushing until it wore itself out. The bottom picture in the image below shows the supporting wall is in place and the elephant (the aggressor) is vanishing!

Image 1

Image 2

During the time I had the vision of the elephant, I had a second vision. It was of an evil mountain. I knew the mountain was evil because it had the smiling face of a wicked person etched on the surface. Suddenly, the mountain began to shake, and it imploded, collapsing in on itself. The evil smile vanished from the face on the mountain as it realized that it was trapped by its own evil.

The mountain vision had the same message as the elephant vision. God used both illustrations to demonstrate His point. Evil eventually buckles under its own schemes. It is not able to prevail! It's not that powerful.

Then, I received these words:

> [D]o not be afraid of them or their words. Do not be afraid, though briers and thorns are all around you and you live among scorpions. Do not be afraid of what they say or be terrified by them... (Ezekiel 2:6, NIV)

> Behold, I have made thy face strong against their faces, and thy forehead strong against their foreheads. (Ezekiel 3:8, KJV)

So, as I stood in the storm, His words strengthened me. "Do not be afraid of what they say or be terrified by them." I would rely on His words in the days ahead. I came to understand, as He was so kind to show, that He was with me in the storm, providing (I felt the Holy Spirit's attention on this) a "wall" of support that would counter the forces pushing in on my life!

This spiritual support is a privilege available to every Kingdom citizen. In this case it is a literal shoring up (I felt the Holy Spirit's attention on this)—a power coming alongside and providing strength and supports that prevent me from being "toppled," that prevents my future from being uprooted. That is an incredible advantage of Kingdom citizenship.

I would learn too, that the storm, the conflict, was allowed into my life for a purpose! I would be different at the end of this (I felt

God's attention on that). I was being fashioned into the woman He had intended me to be, one that relies on Him, and one that comes to realize His love for me (I felt God's attention on that).

The conflict would strengthen our relationship. In other words, by totally and consistently relying on God in times of trouble, God would show Himself strong on my behalf. He would not leave me without support. Those who rely on God are like a strong wall in the face of adversity, and He will never permit the righteous to be moved. As it says in scripture, "Cast your cares on the Lord and he will sustain you; he will never let the righteous be shaken" (Psalm 55:22, NIV).

In other words, that "elephant-size" trouble will not topple your life when you trust in Him (Psalm 55:2, ESV). As He says, "Fear not, for I am with you, be not dismayed, for I am your God. I will strengthen you, I will help you. I will uphold you with my righteous right hand" (Isaiah 41:10, ESV).

David shows us how to rely on God in times of intense conflict. In 1 Samuel, there is a story about David right before he became king. The reigning King Saul was a type of bully, the "elephant" if you will, that hunted David and tried to harass and destroy him. Saul's primary motivator was jealousy.

The Bible says,

> When David returned from killing the Philistine, the women came out of all the cities of Israel, singing and dancing, to meet King Saul... and said, "Saul has killed his thousands, and David his ten thousands." Then, Saul became very angry...And Saul was jealous and did not trust David from that day on. (1 Samuel 18:6–9, NLV)

But the more Saul, the aggressor, hunted David, the weaker Saul became. In 2 Samuel, it states: "The war between the house of Saul and the house of David lasted a long time. David grew stronger and stronger, while the house of Saul grew weaker and weaker" (2

Samuel 3:1, NIV). While Saul was pushing against David and trying to topple his life, he encountered the resisting forces of God because God was with David (see 1 Samuel 18:14).

David grew stronger because he was like that wall in my vision. David might have looked "small" compared to Saul's army, but he had the support and the backing of a great massive God. Therefore, David could not be defeated. Saul was like the elephant in the vision. The more he pushed against David, the more he engaged the resisting forces of the Kingdom of God!

* * * * * * *

The battle against David was spiritual and was rooted in the kingdom of darkness. While Saul was trying to kill David (to prevent him from being king), there were demonic forces in Saul's life with their eyes on a greater prize. The great prize was God's promise to David. "For this is what the Lord says; David will never fail to have a man to sit on the throne of Israel…" (Jeremiah 33:17, NIV). In this scripture, God promises David that his descendants will sit on the throne of Israel forever.

David was being given an eternal dynasty—a rather magnificent prospect culminating with the Christ, with Jesus taking that eternal seat as a fulfillment of promise.[48] Without being fully conscious of what he was doing, Saul was trying to stop David in order to stop the promise, to cut short David's magnificent future and stop the Christ.

So, when Saul hunted David, the fight was against God's eternal promise. That's worth repeating! Sure, Saul wanted to cut David off from the throne, but the underlying battle was to stop that eternal promise from manifesting. A promise that was directly linked to the Messiah.

David was smart to lean on God, being careful not to fight Saul, but to let God handle it. The battle truly did not belong to David, but to God. David simply held his peace and resisted the temptation to strike back, and Saul eventually collapsed under his own evil schemes. "David grew stronger and stronger, while the house of Saul grew weaker and weaker" (2 Samuel 3:1, NIV).

Remember, in 2 Samuel it states: "The war between the house of Saul and house of David lasted a long time." It is worth noting that the *duration* of the battle provided *opportunity* for David. God was using the battle, and the length of time, to prepare David to be king! While on the run and living in the forest, David was being schooled on leading an army, honoring God, and how to be mentally strong in battle.

God allowed David to remain in conflict because He was building David's character, his ability to plan and strategize, and most importantly, He used the moment to build their relationship. David learned to trust God on a greater level.

God didn't shield David from conflict because adversity can be useful. He used Saul's craziness to strengthen David. It was a sort of military school there in the middle of the desert. David was being taught to handle adversity on a smaller scale because God was about to hand over an entire nation to his charge—the tribe of Judah, and later, all of Israel (see 2 Samuel 2).

So, David needed to be courageous! He needed to man up to every challenge. And he needed to learn all he could about his God!

God told David up front that he would be king someday so that when the crazy challenges began, David, in his heart, understood why he was being opposed. He must have known on some level that God was getting him ready. That it was "training day."

While Saul was hunting David, it would have been wise for Saul to do a quick assessment of his own life. He may have noticed that nothing had been going right since he launched his campaign against David. He had failing health, strife in his house, and was looking to a witch for advice (see 1 Samuel 28:7 and 1 Samuel 16). He was tormented. He was declining as David was rising. David was gaining an army, winning battles, his household was increasing, and he was growing stronger in God (see 1 Samuel 18 and 2 Samuel 3:1, 3:2).

It reinforces the vision of the elephant and the wall—that those who oppose the people of God decline over time while the God-centered person increases.

Several years later, when David was ready to be king, Saul collapsed and vanished from the equation. David didn't have to lift a finger against Saul. In the end, it was Saul's evil tactics that did him in, that isolated him from God, and caused his downfall.

* * * * * * *

So, when the devil comes in like a flood, it begs the questions, "What on earth has God got planned that would pull that much opposition? What spiritual destiny is the devil trying to stop?" The strong opposition is trying to block something very, very significant.

And so, confronted by sizable and unpleasant opposition, I wanted to know what God was up to in my life. I closed my eyes and prayed and listened, and I had a vision of my future. The "storm" still raging around me, I could see myself in the future, like a glimpse through a rain cloud. I saw some of what God has in store for me, and it was just for a moment, like a fleeting wind, but it gave me great hope!

By the grace of God, I realize that the trouble I have been facing is nothing in comparison to the future He has in store for me. (I felt God's attention on this!)

The vision of the elephant shows that by abiding in God, I am getting stronger and my opponents are getting weaker; not from anything that I've done, but from their own evil tactics.

* * * * * * *

I have learned in the school of perfect storms that if I stay calm and trust God, then God will show me how to harness the wind and the rain and the sun of it all. What do I mean?

As just one example: my adversary starts an evil and degrading rumor! I get wind if it and might feel disappointed, hurt, or bothered. Instead of retaliating, I go to God and pray for strength (I felt the Holy Spirit's attention on that) to harness my own emotions like a solar panel harnesses the sun—I take control of my emotions, I reign it in, and I refine it until it becomes passion; then I pour that passion into my writing. So, it went from an attack on my character to a creative experience at my computer. Do you see? With the help of God, the storm became my servant!

God is teaching me that anything the enemy sends my way can be harnessed and worked to my advantage. Energy is energy, and even though the enemy might send me "bad" energy, it is still energy, and there is a way to use it for fuel.

The biggest payoff for me from the pressure and opposition is that I've spent so much time with God that He and I have become good friends! I have gotten to the point where I know His "voice," meaning my soul is so finely tuned that I recognize His presence and understand His thoughts toward me (glory to God).

I know when He has me on His mind. Our hearts are connected (I felt the Holy Spirit's attention on this)! I can't begin to imagine the benefit and consequence that incredible connection will have for my future. That advancement in relationship with God was a direct result of my enemies' attacks.

Again, the enemies' tactics drove me to God. That is an enormous payoff! And incredibly important for where God is taking me!

Trailblazer, whatever is confronting you, whatever is seeking to destroy you, don't lose the payoff (I felt the Holy Spirit's attention on this)! Don't let it be in vain. Go to God and find out *why* you are in battle and how you can "cash in." Is He allowing the battle because He is preparing you to be "king"?

Take the "wicked stepsisters" in the Cinderella[49] fairy tale, for example. The wicked sisters were a type of bully to Cinderella. They thought of all types of ways to make her miserable. Cinderella got stuck with all the lousy chores, like cleaning the ashes from the fireplace, and the sisters spoke to her harshly. Nevertheless, Cinderella responded with self-control, and even kindness, the very virtues she would need to be queen. (In fact, each time she encountered the wicked sisters, she was learning how to handle difficult people with grace and poise.)

I dare say that if Cinderella had allowed the foul attitude of the wicked sisters to infect her, if in fact, Cinderella had thrown a punch, or gotten nasty in return, she never would have found favor in the eyes of the prince. Those virtues would be useless, or even dangerous to him. Instead, she maintained a calm demeanor and the right attitude fitting for a queen! It made her stand out to prince charming.

So, you see, your attitude and response in conflict will determine your destiny. Don't get nasty. As a Kingdom citizen, you're better than that! Don't panic. Abide in God and allow him to form great virtues in you—virtues that will be useful when He promotes you. *Wow, that is good stuff Holy Spirit. God is present in this. Thank you, Lord.*

* * * * * *

If you are a Kingdom citizen, someone following after God and committed to serving Him, and find yourself under attack, don't worry. God has you covered! Take a deep breath and trust in Him.

"In fact, everyone who wants to live a godly life in Christ Jesus will be persecuted…" (2 Timothy 3:12, NIV). Welcome to Kingdom citizenship, to walking with Christ, and brace yourself for a victory (I feel the Holy Spirit's attention on this)!

Kingdom citizens have this guarantee: "No weapon that is formed against thee shall prosper; and every tongue that shall rise against thee in judgement thou shalt condemn. This *is* the heritage of the servants of the Lord, and their righteousness is of me, saith the Lord" (Isaiah 54:17, KJV).

Whenever the devil confronts you, it is always opportunity for God to work it to your advantage. God is amazingly good at what He does, and as you trust in Him, you will see for yourself that no weapon formed against a child of God can prosper! God will show up and show you how to be unstoppable! Shout somebody!

Again, don't let the longevity of the conflict phase you because it also corresponds to the magnitude of what God has in store for you.

So what sort of opposition is in your "face"? Remember, abide in God!

In our story, David had Jonathan as an ally, but often, it might just be you and God. Fortunately, that is more than enough. God is a true friend in a storm—your strongest ally!

And whatever you do, don't quit your faith! God is not the problem; He is the solution. And with His help, you will make it through that storm and come out stronger for it!

Serving God doesn't make us immune to storms. In life, it will rain on the just and unjust (see Matthew 5:45), but how fortunate for those who trust in the Lord that we have the Creator on our side.

41

Kingdom Privileges

Visa-Free Travel

Heaven is a rich and generous place; and as a citizen of the Kingdom, one has the privilege of visiting without a visa! In scripture, Jesus tells believers, "You know the way to the place where I am going" (John 14:4, NIV). That seems to suggest that those born of God have a built in GPS wired for Heaven. I went to such an enchanting place on at least two occasions.

I remember once walking along a path in Heaven. It was magical, with trees towering overhead. Then I saw someone walking toward me. She was lovely and had a sense of regality about her. As I got closer, I saw that it was my sister. She looked so different; I couldn't help but stare at her. Here on Earth, she is partially paralyzed on one side, walks with a limp, and suffers from seizures and sickle cell anemia.

Yet in Heaven, I didn't recognize her at first because there is no sickness in Heaven. By the grace of God, all the twisting from polio, the weariness from seizures, and the wrinkles from years of pain were swept away and what remained was lovely!

In another vision, I saw myself in a horse drawn carriage, driving along the outskirts of a harbor with my grandmother seated beside me. It was a sunny day and again; the weather was perfect. I suppose there were other ways to get around, but we seemed to enjoy our ride in the open-top carriage; and there were people by the harbor, coming and going, and it was perfectly peaceful.

In these visions, I got a glimpse of myself functioning as a citizen of Heaven and experiencing one aspect of the enormous Kingdom of God—a life without sin and pain. I felt alive with meaning and had an incredible sense of well-being. (I felt the Holy Spirit on that.)

When one accepts Jesus as Lord, a new birth occurs. That person transitions from death to life, and the "life" is multi-layered and extraordinary. You get amazing access to a place you would never believe until you see it for yourself! (I sense God's attention on this.)

Kingdom citizen, Heaven is your home.

42

Kingdom Privileges

Sword of the Spirit

I was in the rathskeller, a little tavern on the college campus that sold nonalcoholic beverages, when I noticed a commotion at one of the tables. A woman, looking very much like an old gypsy, was reading palms. The young naive students, including me, flocked around the table, each intrigued by the prospect of getting a glimpse into our uncertain future.

Finally, it was my turn. I, seated across from trouble, was about to meet up with the power of sin! As she looked into the palm of my hands, she paused.

Suddenly, I felt a bit uneasy. "Don't tell me anything bad," I said.

She was thinking, brewing up an evil message. Then she opened her mouth and breathed out what she saw in the dark parts of her mind: "You will lose your first child," she told me. Then she added, "Otherwise, your life will be fine."

My friend Bobby was next to step into her trap. "You will lose a finger," she told him.

As Bobby and I walked back to the dorms, the old woman's words rang in my mind like a cemetery bell. She released a curse over my life, and though Bobby laughed about what she told him about losing a finger, I could tell that there was some nervousness and uncertainty in his voice as well. We were so naive and unguided that we allowed a witch to speak over us.

We had no idea what we were dealing with at the time and ran into a "wall" of evil words. My cultural island background and my teenage years left me thinking that people like the old gypsy witch knew what they were talking about; that their word was law.

The witch was a wordsmith, a mouthpiece of the devil, equipped with curses and hoping to pollute the future of anyone who was naive enough to step into her trap.

She didn't show up in the rathskeller that day by accident or for some casual reason. She was on assignment! She was sent by the devil to weave "crown of thorns" for the students to wear.

* * * * * * *

The "devil's crown of thorns" is used here to describe the deliberate attack the devil launches on the minds of individuals to frighten them and undermine their future.

The devil weaves crown of thorns for those standing at a crossroads. So for example, a witch shows up in a room filled with college students at a time when they are about to step into the future God has for them—when they are most impressionable and vulnerable—and fills their heads with curses, lies, and images of failure. That describes the "devil's crown of thorns." It is meant to burden and pollute the mind and discourage the individual at important junctures in life.

In other words, the sum of all the evil that confronts our thought life, if it were to be given a shape, might resemble a crown of thorns (I feel Jesus's attention on this). "Crown of thorns" are created with the enemy's words and thoughts!

So the devil might pick up a strand of fear words and weave it in with some discouraging words and add to it a few weeds of doubt, which he intends to rest on the head of the "victim" in the form of a mental attack.

So how does one destroy the thorny crown? (I felt the Holy Spirit's attention on that.) Later in life, long after that event in the rathskeller, I would learn that God has a solution for breaking curses—for obliterating the crown of thorns!

The answer to the devil's mental bombardment is the sword of the Spirit (I felt the Holy Spirit's attention on that). Every word the devil releases, every curse can be broken by applying the sword, also known as the word of God.

As it says in scripture: "[T]ake… the sword of the Spirit, which is the word of God. Pray in the Spirit at all times, with every kind of prayer and petition…" (Ephesians 6:17, 16–18). You "take" the sword of the Spirit by putting God's word into your mouth and speaking it over your situation.

Answer every threat to your health, to your future, and to your family with the Word of God! What does God say about your situation? That's the only thing that matters!

As a Kingdom citizen, you get the privilege of speaking God's Word over your life, resisting the negative suggestions that pop into your mind, resist those thoughts of doubt, limitation, and failure that the devil sends your way! Speak God's Word at that thorny crown, and see that situation transform.

Take David for example, from the story of David and Goliath. David was a master at using the sword of the Spirit in battle.

When the story opens, Israel and the Philistines are at war. "The Philistines occupied one hill and the Israelites another, with the valley between them" (1 Samuel 17:3, NIV). Goliath, a ten-foot giant in heavy armor, is of the Philistine army; and David, a teenager with no apparent armor, is with the army of Israel.

The battle begins with a war of words. Goliath mouths off first with the goal of creating a crown of thorns for David to wear. The crown's assignment is to weaken David's mind with fear, threat of disaster, intimidation, and distress.

"He said to David, 'Am I a dog, that you come at me with sticks?' And the Philistine cursed David by his gods. 'Come here,' he said, 'and I will give your flesh to the birds and the wild animals'" (1 Samuel 17:43–44, NIV).

Those evil words Goliath weaved were sent to prepare David for destruction. They were the words the devil was hoping David would wear like a crown on his head and submit to the authority of those words. The devil sent his words ahead of his intentions and Goliath was his mouth peace. But the devil's words hit a "wall" of resistance!

What happened next was amazing! David sent the sword of the Spirit—the Word of God at Goliath. David is about to obliterate the devil's crown of thorns with the sword of the Spirit!

David said:

> You come against me with sword and spear and javelin, but I come against you in the name of the Lord Almighty, the God of the armies of Israel, whom you have defied. This day the Lord will deliver you into my hands, and I'll strike you down and cut off your head. This very day I will give the carcasses of the Philistine army to the birds and the wild animals, and the whole world will know that there is a God in Israel. All those gathered here will know that it is not by sword or spear that the Lord saves; for the battle is the Lord's, and he will give all of you into our hands. (1 Samuel 17:45–47, NIV)

David was confronting Goliath under God's authority and direction; he was speaking God's words at the giant! He was using the sword of the Spirit (I felt the Holy Spirit's attention on that). The word of God had gone forth announcing that the battle belonged to Him, and that the Philistine army would be defeated. David was God's mouthpiece to deliver that message; and God's word would not return to Him void but would fulfill its mission (see Isaiah 55:11).

The clock began ticking for Goliath; it was just a matter of time before God's Word would manifest around him. The young shepherd boy only had a slingshot and a rock to put in that sling to hurl at the giant, but there was more—something was transpiring in the supernatural. The Kingdom of God had come alongside David. God was present!

At that moment on the battlefield, David probably looked at the Philistine army, trying to make eye contact. "All those gathered here will know," he said, "that there is a God in Israel." He wasn't just aiming for Goliath (I felt God's attention on that); he was after the entire army (I felt the Holy Spirit's attention on that).

Notice too that he said, the battle is the "Lord's." Great perspective! He knew the fight wasn't his, but rather, God would engage and defeat Goliath. That stone that David whirled toward Goliath's head was fueled by the words released with it. The stone didn't go alone. It was obeying what God, through David, had already spoken! The words of David—the words of God—gave the stone an assignment!

Goliath had no idea that the little shepherd kid was small on the outside but had a massive Kingdom behind him.

It was the Kingdom of God (represented by David) and the kingdom of darkness (represented by Goliath) at war! The Kingdom possessing the more power-backed words would win!

> As the Philistine moved closer to attack him, David ran quickly toward the battle line to meet him. Reaching into his bag and taking out a stone, he slung it and struck the Philistine on the forehead. The stone sank into his forehead, and he fell face down on the ground... David ran and stood over him. He took hold of the Philistine's sword and drew it from the sheath. After he killed him, he cut off his head with the sword. When the Philistines saw that their hero was dead, they turned and ran. Then the men of Israel and Judah surged forward with a shout and pursued the Philistines..." (1 Samuel 17:48–52, NIV)

David didn't stop to ponder Goliath's words. He simply released God's words and went to work with the ministry God had given him to do in that moment, which was to release the stone in a sling (I felt God's attention on this) and trust God to do the rest.

This demonstrates that the devil's crown of thorns is no match for the sword of the Spirit (I felt the Holy Spirit's attention on this).

* * * * * * *

David shows us that an efficient response to the devil's crown of thorns will always be the sword of the Spirit! Speak God's Word in faith at the situation and let that settle it! "For the word of God is alive and active. Sharper than any double-edged sword" (Hebrews 4:12, NIV).

What does God say? That's all that matters! The best way to remain mentally guarded is to stay close to God. Speak only what God says—reject the devil's suggestions and lies—focus on the proven, unfailing word of God (I felt the Holy Spirit's attention on this).

It is a matter of whose report do you believe. (I felt the Holy Spirit's attention on that.) Do you quake at the devil's words, or do you recall the word of God? Do you wield the sword of the Spirt at the devil, or do you buckle in fear and worry?

Kingdom citizen, the Word of God is one of your most powerful weapons!

* * * * * *

We can apply the sword of the Spirit to our lives on an individual level and on a corporate level. So for example, when you walk into a church and find that the congregation is totally preoccupied with battling the devil on a mental level, you understand that the crown of thorns the devil sent their way is keeping them in a constant state of mental conflict. The devil has their full attention and keeps them fearful so that every Sunday they need to be "delivered" and "re-delivered."

On the other hand, if you walk into a church and you find that people are busy about God's work: combatting child trafficking, feeding the homeless, spreading the gospel of Jesus Christ (I feel the Holy Spirit's attention on this), then you know that they are Kingdom minded!

Their focus is the word of God and what God has given them to do in the moment. Like David, they are not giving weight to the devil's words; they are fully focused on God.

The crown of thorns the devil sent their way did not penetrate their minds, is not affecting their thoughts, is not wasting their time. (I felt God's attention on this.) They are walking in true victory, completing their God given assignment, staying focused on the word of God, and championing their way through life. They are experiencing true Kingdom living!

Acknowledging the word of God and fully focusing on the *power* of salvation in Jesus Christ will always be much more effective (I feel the Holy Spirit's attention on this) and powerful than spending hours and days rebuking the devil and engaging the devil in mental battles.

If you are struggling to break free from the devil's "crown of thorns," if the devil has you in a mental state of constant worry and anxiety, take it to God in prayer. Let God fortify your emotions and thought life to reject the crown's influence.

As you read the Bible, the word of God will build you up in your mind and remind you of who you are. This fortification is the work of the Holy Spirit (I feel the Holy Spirit's attention on this). In other words, you are not in the battle alone; God is here to help. He has given you His word! And the more you learn to rely on and trust in His Word, the stronger you will become!

As God promises His servants: "No weapon formed against you shall prosper, and every tongue which rises against you in judgement you shall condemn..." (I felt the Holy Spirit's attention on that).

"This is the heritage of the servants of the Lord, and their righteousness is of Me,' Says the Lord" (Isaiah 54:17, NKJV).

So, you see, the Word of God is a powerful tool; and amazingly, it is just one piece of the "armor" available to every Kingdom citizen!

> Finally, be strong in the Lord and in his mighty power. Put on the full armor of God, so that you can take your stand against the devil's schemes…Stand firm then, with the belt of truth…the breastplate of righteousness in place, and…the gospel of peace. Take the helmet of salvation and the sword of the Spirit, which is the word of God. And pray in the Spirit on all occasions… (Ephesians 6:10–18, NIV)

Each piece of armor will guard and protect you from the devil's trickery.

* * * * * * *

Later in life, when I accepted Jesus as Lord and began to realize the power and authority I have as a citizen of the Kingdom of God, I circled back to that moment in the rathskeller. I revisited it in my mind, sat again before the witch; but this time, I was a different person—I had a few tools under my belt. My faith in God had grown to the point where I could confront (I see the devil's attention on this) the devil's curse.

Equipped with the Word of God (I felt the Holy Spirit's attention on that) and the rest of my spiritual armor, I confessed my faith in God's promises for my life and condemned the devil's evil words. I released the Word of God against the devil's crown of thorns and watched it transform my future!

Being able to use the sword of the Spirit (and the entire full armor) is an incredible privilege available to every citizen of the Kingdom!

43

Kingdom Privilege

Proper Identity

When I read the story about Oksana[50] (based on actual events) during one of my law school exams, my heart sank. In my imagination, I could picture the torment the young woman endured. Oksana was the victim of identity homicide.

Her story went something like this: While traveling to and from school, three girls, Mary, Suzanne, and Frances (not actual names) would gather around their schoolmate, Oksana, at the bus stop, push the books from her hands, and call her slut and loser.

They told her that she was trash and didn't belong in this country, and that if she ever came around their neighborhood that she would be "sorry." This went on for months and months until finally, Oksana hung herself in her room.

The implication in the story was that Oksana did not invite or instigate any of the trouble she experienced. It was also implied that the school did nothing to help her; that her teachers did not intervene.

My job, during the exam, was to determine what the legal issues were, what recourse the parents might have, and to determine the responsibility and liability of all the parties. After a "practical" analysis and discussion, I took time to privately consider the spiritual side of the problem, and from a scriptural perspective.

* * * * * *

In the beginning of the story, Oksana was a kid with a lot of promise. Then, she met three girls who didn't like what they saw, who perhaps experienced waves of jealousy, or maybe they were just trained to destroy anything that showed up in their world that resembled greatness. Whatever it was, they weaved a plot to destroy her life.

The three teens made it their mission to re-define Oksana; to convince her and anyone who would listen to them that Oksana was bad news. The bullies probably sat up at night thinking of the best words and phrases to use in their re-definition process.

Perhaps the bullies understood that she was clever at some things, so they may have felt that the best word to use to re-define her was to call her "stupid." And on and on it went until finally Oksana buckled under the pressure! Apparently, she had no one around to counter the attacks, to remind her of who she actually was, and so she gave up—exactly what the bullies wanted. Exactly what the devil wanted!

The redefinition of Oksana was a move by demonic forces and the bullies were the willing tools that they used. The bottom line is that God never intended for Oksana to die prematurely. He never intended for her to take her own life before her destiny could be realized and her gifts manifested. She was a victim of identity homicide—one of the devil's key tactics.

The devil also managed to destroy the lives of the three teens: Mary, Frances and Suzanne, who after that day will have to live with their role in Oksana's death.

Jesus, in His mercy, offers grace to people like Oksana—the oddballs—the one's sitting alone in the cafeteria leaning over a plate of macaroni and cheese. Those little galaxies of genius that just don't seem to fit in. God has a plan for everyone's life and has a way of assimilating everyone who feels like an outcast by wrapping His arms around them, by engrafting them into His Kingdom, by giving them a future and a hope (see Jeremiah 29:11).

God was on standby, hoping, I can only imagine, that Oksana would lean on Him, and trust Him to navigate her destiny. Perhaps He would have told her to keep her eyes on Him, and He might have taken her by the hand and led her to understand who she is, and the amazing future He had in store for her. That is His nature, but the bullies made a lot of noise and ran an effective demonic interference.

* * * * * * *

Was Oksana destined to become a brilliant concert pianist who raised millions for the fight against child trafficking? Or was she destined to run for prime minister or president of her country, and change the wave of poverty into a meaningful and robust society? Why did the devil single her out?

When Oksana met up with the bullies, she was at a crossroads. Was she a piano aficionado with an eye on the Julliard School of Music; or the first to go to college in her family, opening doors to the generations that would follow? Whatever it was, on the way to fulfilling her future, she encountered a massive distraction (I felt the Holy Spirit's attention on this) that derailed her life and her life abruptly ended.

Oksana experienced a flood of distractions and assaults. The bullies were like little hyenas that found her each school day and bickered at her continually. They had her attention and would use the opportunity to fill her head with lies and fear, in order to distort her self-image.

But the real enemy was not the bullies, but the spirit behind them. "For our struggle is not against flesh and blood, but against the rulers, against the authorities, against the powers of this dark world and against the spiritual forces of evil in the heavenly realms" (Ephesians 6:12, NIV).

While the bullies were attempting to redefine Oksana, God, if allowed, would counter with His own definition process by introducing Oksana to His image of her. He saw her as someone wonderfully and fearfully made, for example (see Psalm 139:14).

* * * * * *

God in His mercy extends forgiveness and redemption to the bullies, not wanting anyone to perish. (See 2 Peter 3:9.) It doesn't mean the girls are free of the consequences of participating in the torment of another human being; it means God can bring salvation to all parties somehow—specifically through the person of Jesus.

So, God is interested in the re-definition of the bullies. He wants to change their self-perception and provide a vision of what they can become. Only God could wield such results; only He could show that much mercy!

God is here to save anyone who will say "yes" to Jesus for we are all guilty of some form of sin; we are all in need of mercy. By accepting Jesus, we come across an accurate definition of who we are and begin to develop a healthy vision for the future (see Psalm 139:14).

The Kingdom of God therefore provides a complete answer to both sides of the issue by extending salvation to *all* parties, and in that place of salvation, a new identity begins to develop. Over time, the aggressive bully and the timid victim both begin to look more like God because the Spirit of God is in them and the nature of God is being developed in them. And "the fruit of the Spirit is love, joy, peace, forbearance, kindness, goodness, faithfulness" (Galatians 5:22, NIV).

In Oksana's case, this new identity rooted in the Kingdom of God would help her to respond (I felt the Holy Spirit's attention on that) to the bullies from a position of power instead of a position of fear. Her sense of *acceptance* in the powerful Kingdom of God, followed by a healthy identity in Christ, would begin her journey of empowerment.

* * * * * *

Let's look at this another way. Its movie night featuring *The Lion King*.[51] This Disney movie demonstrates why a bully (a person with a devilish assignment) appears on the scene and what they aim to accomplish.

The movie opens with Mufasa, the Lion King, presenting his newborn cub, Simba, to his kingdom. Mufasa rules the Pride Lands, a rich stretch of green jungle filled with lions, giraffes, and elephants, but it also has hyenas and Mufasa's menacing brother, Scar.

Scar and the hyenas are the bullies in this drama, and their goal is to kill, steal, and destroy! Scar wants to kill Mufasa and steal the throne and destroy Simba's future as king.

Later in the movie, after Scar kills Mufasa, he pins the blame on Simba; then he convinces Simba to run away from the Pride Lands (and from his future as king). The moment Simba is out of the scene, Scar begins to destroy the Pride Lands.

While trying to forget his past, Simba has a spiritual encounter with his father, Mufasa, who challenges him to stop running and to take his rightful place as king. "You have forgotten who you are," Mufasa tells Simba. "You are more than what you have become. You must take your place in the circle of life. Remember who you are." With that encounter and the help of his friends, Simba returns to the Pride Lands to confront Scar!

A battle ensues and Simba unseats Scar and claims his throne as the Lion King!

* * * * * * *

When a person has a great future ahead, a bully often appears on the scene to try to distort their identity and block their future.

Our little lion cub in *The Lion King* nearly lost his throne to a devilish Uncle Scar when he believed his uncle's lies and saw himself as something he was not. Scar was successful for a time in re-defining Simba as a failure and convincing him to run and hide. But then Simba has a special encounter with Mufasa who reminded him that he was more than he had become and encouraged him to return to the Pride Lands to take his rightful place as king.

Sadly, bully encounters often lack a fairytale ending, as seen in Oksana's case. The bullies were successful in convincing her that her promising life was worthless. As a result, she took her own life. This is unfortunately the story for many teens (and adults) around the world. If only they would realize how much God loves them, how incredibly valuable their lives are, and the amazing plans God has in store for them (I felt God's attention on that). He sees them as fearfully and wonderfully made, for example, and wants to give them a future and a hope (see Jeremiah 29:11).

* * * * * * *

A real-life example of God at work in the life of a teenager to defeat the devil's re-definition process (I felt God's attention on that) is the life of David, the shepherd boy He called to be king of Israel. (See 1 Samuel 16.)

And indeed, David would be given the throne one day, but on the journey, he would encounter several bullies intent on stopping him, including Goliath, the giant from Gath!

Goliath was much larger and older than David and used his size and experience in battle to try to frighten David; he cursed David and tried to define him as powerless and useless. In other words, while God was calling David a future king, Goliath was, in effect, calling David a fly to be squashed! (See 1 Samuel 17.)

David's future would depend on who he chose to believe! Fortunately, David didn't listen to Goliath's words about him; instead, he chose to believe God! He wasn't relying on his own strength; he was relying on the strength and power of God to give him the victory! David showed faith in God, confident that with God by his side, he could indeed be king!

His God-centered approach cut short the devil's schemes, and with God's help, he was able to get the victory over Goliath and step into his future as king!

Now each one of us gets to choose the ending of our own story. We get to decide who defines us and impacts our future! Again, the devil doesn't get the privilege of defining who you are (I felt the Holy Spirit's attention on that) when you are part of the family of God.

When the bully approaches, focus on God, and remember who you are—created in God's image to rule over your circumstances.

And God will give you strategies for holding onto what belongs to you, whether it be a marriage, or a ministry, or relationship with God (I feel the Holy Spirit's attention on this)! The devil can't steal your future when you trust in God.

44

Kingdom Privilege

Inclusion

Kentucky blue-grass region, late 1800s. A mist covers a small town with a country store, a tailor's shop, and a saloon backed up to the side of a mountain. Coming into frame, the front door of the country store with cracks and holes from years of use. The door opens slowly and reveals—

A fifteen-year old Hispanic boy, Bobby, staring at the picture of a thoroughbred nailed to the wall. Behind him, Sam, the grocer, is fetching his Momma's groceries.

"Nice horse, ain't it?" Sam says, while forcing a bag of rice into a brown paper bag.

"Sure is." Bobby smiles, still staring at the picture.

Suddenly, a skinny black teen rushes in, stops in the doorway, breathless. He looks worried. When he finally catches his breath, he blurts out to Bobby, "You heard?"

In the very next scene, we see Bobby running through the woods, turning in circles and calling out the name of his best friend, "Danny!"

Suddenly, he stops and stares at a form in the distance hanging from a tree. He takes off running toward it but slows when he realizes it's Danny.

The color drains from his face, and he's sweating as he reaches up and cradles Danny's bare feet in his hands.

* * * * * * *

It's the deep south at a time when black boys are hunted down and hanged for menial things like talking back. Danny was caught and hanged by the notorious Woodford brothers.

When Bobby found Danny in the woods, it was as if his heart broke open and a world of pain rushed in and got locked in his chest. His eyes filled with tears. He wished he had gotten there sooner, wished he could undo the tragedy hanging before him.

He climbs onto a tree limb and cuts the rope from around Danny's neck. Then, while choking back tears, he jumps off the tree and rolls Danny onto his back to keep the dust off his face.

A week later, while walking through the woods, Bobby hears a sound coming from the bush. He walks over, parts a few tree limbs and is shocked by what he sees—a thoroughbred, a jet-black colt named Eminence, tied up alone in the shade. A spark returns to his eyes as he stares at the racehorse.

He can't hardly believe it. He's never seen a horse so glossy and tall with bright white hoofs. A smile escapes from his face as he walks over and begins to circle the racehorse, patting the side of the horse as he goes.

At that moment, outside the stables on that Sunday afternoon, Bobby promises himself that one day he would ride Eminence. But there is only one thing standing in his way—the racehorse belongs to the Woodford boys, the guys that killed Danny.

Later, in a strange twist of fate, there's an opening at Woodford Stables for a boy to "hot walk" Eminence after each race (to help the horse cool down), but being a hot walker would mean facing that pain trapped in his chest; it would mean working for the people who killed his best friend, and it would mean facing his fear that he too might end up like Danny.

His mother, Beth, sees the answer is clear. Bobby won't take the job. But Tryfeena, Bobby's grandmother, gets alone with God in her cabin nestled in the Kentucky blue grass, and she weeps and she prays.

In the middle of her prayer, she receives a vision. It was just for a split second, but she sees something that convinces her that Bobby's destiny is tied to Eminence.

"They not gonna kill Bobby," she says, referring to the Woodford boys that stalk the bush every night. "And Bobby is gonna take that job at the stables."

In her mind, that settles it! She then takes on the mission of convincing Bobby that he has it in him to be a hot walker, even if it means working for the Woodfords.

But the Woodford boys have Bobby's ear and tell him every chance they get that he will end up just like Danny. They mock and taunt him to tears.

Now, Tryfeena must teach Bobby to pray and tame his thinking, to trust the outcome to God and to go fearlessly toward his future!

* * * * * * * *

My screenplay, *The Jockey*, is based on historical events of the late 1800s where boys of "color" were given the best mounts to ride in horse races because no one else wanted the job. They became strong riders, able to handle the horse in speed, and cross the finish line in record time. As horse racing became a lucrative sport, they were gradually pushed out of the scene.

But in the middle of all the rejection and chaos, one Hispanic family saw opportunity. If they could be strong in the face of racism and muster up enough courage to trust God and reach for their dreams, it would change everything! And in that place of trusting God, they find the strength to forgive, and the *power* to live the life God intended. (I felt the Holy Spirit's attention on that.)

* * * * * * *

Rejection is a horrible and painful experience! We have all felt it at one point or another, some more than most. Somehow, I think

Bobby tells our story—anyone who has ever felt rejected or wounded because of the color of their skin or because they live in poverty.

So when God finds us as we go through life, we might feel very much like the character in *The Jockey*, beat up and maybe rejected (I feel Jesus's attention on that).

Jesus understands this plight—the pain of being ostracized just because of one's race. He too was rejected while He walked the earth. He said that His home is not of this world or people would have received Him, but the religious leaders during His time on Earth hated Him because He was different (see John 15:18; see also John 1:11).

What Jesus experienced might be akin to a type of racism. He dealt with it by remembering why He came to Earth and by praying for those who hate him, understanding that the devil is behind all acts of hate (see Luke 17:1–6; see also Ephesians 6:12). "For we do not wrestle against flesh and blood, but against principalities, against powers, against the rulers of the darkness of this age, against spiritual *hosts* of wickedness in the heavenly *places*" (Ephesians 6:12, NKJV).

Jesus presents the solution (I felt the Holy Spirit's attention on that) to the rejection that confronts us. "Seek first the Kingdom of God," He urges everyone. There you will find acceptance and peace, and in that place of inclusion and acceptance, you find the courage and strength to respond properly to rejection. You find the strength to respond and not react—to forgive and to not let a culture of rejection cut short the destiny God has in store for you.

* * * * * * *

The Kingdom of God has a *culture* of forgiveness and inclusion. That, in my opinion, is one of the most powerful and attractive aspects of the Kingdom—the ability to help everyone feel wanted. All who accept Jesus as Lord are transformed by the power of the Holy Spirit into "new" creatures and become part of the Kingdom as citizens. Whatever our history, God brings forgiveness, repair, and inclusion.

A lot of people are struggling to fit in *somewhere*. Some churches are notorious for having cliques and being somewhat exclusive. But that is not the culture of the Kingdom of God. In the Kingdom, you are loved and invited. You are wanted! "…God does not show favoritism" (Acts 10:34, NIV). Which means He loves you as much as the other citizens of His Kingdom. You matter to God. Jesus demonstrates this by dying on the cross so that *everyone* could be saved! (See 2 Corinthians 5:15.)

The will of God is that no one should perish, that no one should be excluded (see 2 Peter 3:9). No matter your race, social status, or how much money you have in your pocket, God extends this opportunity to be saved (I felt the Holy Spirit's attention on that).

In our story, Bobby is a kid with a big dream—to ride Eminence in the Derby! But he's up against a formidable foe—a few boys who hate him. Black boys were falling off radar and found lynched in the Kentucky woods, and he was an energetic kid and quick to talk back. He was a recipe for disaster.

Then he learned how to pray (I felt the Holy Spirit's attention on that), showing a spiritual law at work—prayer is the one thing that gets Heaven to work on your behalf. And in that place of prayer, he finds the acceptance his soul craved. He found too (I felt God's attention on this) the power and courage needed to forgive his haters and stand up for his dream.

Like Bobby, you may have experienced a lot of rejection in life because of your skin color. Or maybe you were caught up in all types of sin and feel unworthy, but whatever your past, you can start anew (I felt the Holy Spirit's attention on that).

You are invited! God wants *you* as part of the Kingdom and promises His citizens a future and a hope (see Jeremiah 29:11).

The first step is the prayer of salvation.

45

Kingdom Privilege

The Name of Jesus

Recently, as I was combing my hair, I noticed several strands coming out at once. It was the result of coloring my hair too soon after a perm, so it was falling out more than usual and the sight of it startled me! Without thinking, I blurted out, "Jesus, help me!" What happened next surprised me! I felt His instant full attention. I was quiet for a second as I stood there with strands of hair in a small pile near my feet.

At that moment, He might have inspected me from head to toe for some emergency or looked around my room to see if perhaps there had been some intrusion, but really, it was just my hair.

I felt foolish. Losing some strands of hair just didn't seem like reason enough to blurt out His name. "Forgive me, Lord," I said. "It's just my hair."

On one hand, I wasn't being fickle. I am a black woman with curly roots to my hair and it takes a lot of work to grow and keep healthy; so, it was difficult to see it falling out. Nevertheless, in comparison to what's happening in the world, it didn't seem to warrant calling on the name of Jesus with such urgency.

When I noticed His response, I felt a little silly but also very grateful and reassured that He would respond so quickly to my call, however misplaced, and it taught me to be careful how I use His name. He *does* care immensely, and it does get His attention when those in His charge call on Him. So, it is important not to take His name in vain. (I felt the Holy Spirit's attention on that.)

His name is so powerful, that the sound of it makes demons tremble. His name is timeless and has such enormous effect because it belongs to Him—a King, the Son of God. His strong name opens doors, saves souls, delivers from destruction; it has fantastic power in the spirit and physical realm (see Acts 2:21 and Mark 16:17-18)

Hollywood has caught onto the value of strong characters with great names built on a lifetime of integrity and honor, and many of our favorite movies take advantage of this appeal. Take for example, the 2000 blockbuster, *The Gladiator*, a period piece set in second century Rome, released by DreamWorks Pictures.

* * * * * * *

Coming into frame, the main character, Maximus Meridius, a strong and respected general in the Roman army, is getting ready to step into a scorching hot coliseum for a bloody battle. We see him focused, turning in circles, looking at the blood-thirsty cheering crowd that fill the coliseum from one end to the next.

One of the spectators is the malicious and creepy Commodus, Emperor of Rome. We know from the beginning of the movie that Commodus killed his own father, the reigning Emperor, and stole the throne. When Maximus, a beloved friend of the former Emperor protests, Commodus orders his soldier to kill him.

The soldiers manage to kill Maximus's family, but Maximus escapes, only to be caught by slave traders and sold into slavery as a gladiator. That's how he ended up in the middle of the coliseum waiting for fury to unleash. That would be his life day after day as he goes from one battle to the next as a gladiator/slave, performing for a blood thirsty crowd.

In the middle of his torment, he manages to make friends with a trusted, cool-tempered African named Juba.

Juba, a quiet, insightful guy, catches on pretty quickly, and realizes that crazy-Commodus is trying to kill Maximus because he (Maximus) has a very strong name (and influence) among the Roman people. So Juba tells Maximus, "Kill your name before it kills you."

Juba understands that all the trouble plaguing Maximus is linked to his great name. Maximus—each letter and syllable—even the very sound says "strength and power," but it goes beyond that. The name is powerful because the person of Maximus has character, physical strength, and leadership skills that are unmatched in Rome.

He has developed a great name for himself; one that causes the people of Rome, who see him as a great warrior, to love and admire him. That name also causes people like the selfish and sadistic Commodus to feel threatened and to hate him.

(Bear with me. I'll tie this into the gospel in a minute.)

Juba reasons that if Maximus could get rid of his great name or "kill his name," then the pressure would fall away. Maximus could go incognito and escape the enormous responsibility that comes with his name and may even escape Commodus and his wicked attempts to kill him.

However, Maximus realizes that he cannot give up his name because it is linked to his purpose. To fulfill his purpose, he needs a great name, since a great purpose requires a great name—a name that implies honor, strength, and integrity. If he abandoned his name, he would lose his soul, his identity. He would blend in with millions of nameless faces around the world and his purpose would vanish along with him.

His purpose, his dream, is to deliver all of Rome from Commodus's oppression. He has a powerful name that triggers faith, respect and confidence in the people of Rome, but he faces a paradox. He is a slave, no longer a general of the Roman army.

The pressure coming against Maximus is to intimidate him and cause him to abandon his *purpose* (or "kill his name"), to quit and hide from his calling. That would make Commodus very happy, but those who believe in Maximus know that the one thing he must do is to continue to move toward his purpose. Otherwise, the consequence would be unbearable—all of Rome falling to the tyranny of Commodus.

At the end of the story, we see Maximus in the middle of a Roman colosseum, about to confront Commodus, with thousands watching. After some struggle between Maximus and Commodus, and a list of Hollywood special effects, we see that Maximus, bearing his name, overpowers Commodus. Lots of cheers flow from the stands in the coliseum as Maximus finally ends Commodus's reign and his wicked tactics—an act that frees all of Rome.

The light goes on in the theatre as our movie ends.

* * * * * * *

Although I don't endorse the violence in *The Gladiator*, I found it well written with much to think about.

I think that story hits on a familiar theme—the resistance we often encounter as we move toward purpose (I felt Jesus's attention on that). Sometimes, it seems all hell breaks loose.

As long as we are willing to remain mental slaves to mediocrity and complacency, then we manage to stay alive in a little mundane existence, but stepping out in faith is a huge challenge.

Yet, Jesus shows us how to live a purpose-driven life. He shows us how to stay the course and fulfill purpose in spite of all the risks. In His case, the road to purpose would mean going to the cross and dying a painful death for all humanity. He had opportunity to quit, yet He stayed the course, steely, determined, in spite of knowing the high price He would have to pay. In the process, His name became great among the people.

Let's go back to our imaginary theatre and see how the Lord of lords lived out His purpose and honored His name in spite of massive trouble.

* * * * * * *

A light flashes across the screen, then the screen fades out in the theater and goes to black and slowly fades in on—

An overhead shot of a Man dressed in a dusty white garment, walking outside Jerusalem with twelve guys. They stop some miles away on the hill that overlooks the city.

The camera pans left and circles from that overhead shot to a close-up of the Person, Jesus. We hold our breath as we stare at His face, taking it all in: the sweat on His brow, that look in His eyes filled with compassion, determination, and things we can't explain, some source of power (I felt the Holy Spirit's attention on this).

Suddenly, we hear a drum, a beat, then a Christian rapper's voice fading into the scene (singing praises to God) while Jesus and the twelve walk toward Jerusalem.

As the rapper's voice tapers off, we get a close-up of Jesus walking through the narrow cobble stoned streets of Jerusalem with amazing humility, pouring out love to a blind man sitting cross-legged on the ground (see John 9:1–12). Instantly, his eyes open and he sees the gentle smile of the Messiah! Then, like popcorn going off all around Him, He causes a crippled man to walk (see John 5), breaks the grip of the devil off of a person's life by casting out a demon (see Matthew 12:22), and on and on it goes.

He is out of control, and He is in control. No one does stuff like this, no ordinary man; and the crowd is weeping, some in shock, soaking in their new freedom—the liberation they feel inside—that breakthrough that they just can't explain! Some are beginning to chant His name as He walks by, "Jesus. Jesus."

"That's the one they call Messiah," they say in soft whispers.

As His name cuts through the streets, somehow arriving in each location before He does, He stays focused on His purpose. He has one key message, and He shares it with anyone who is smart enough to listen. He announces the Kingdom of God is at hand (I felt the Holy Spirit's attention on that). He is telling people about the Kingdom of God! In other words, God's reign and dominion and power is crashing into earth's atmosphere and changing lives!

But this reality of a "Kingdom" frightens the religious leaders who hate the idea of anyone in power besides them. So they plot to kill Jesus, hoping to cut short His message and shut down this notion of a heavenly Kingdom.

Later, with the camera angle showing a long shot of Jesus relaxing with His disciples next to a fire, laughter filling the air, good food and humor, lots of hummus and pita bread, we know that we are observing the unfolding of something that we just can't fully explain.

Because of this incredible and amazing Guy and the Name He carries, everyone's life is changing! Those who believe in His name catch the Spirit, and they too are able to open blind eyes by the power of God!

* * * * * * *

The next day, there is a beat, a tap on a drum, and a rapper singing in the background as we get an overhead shot of Jesus walking through a crowd, touching the heads of children, healing crippled legs, and even healing the leprosy of those that snuck into the crowd—taking them by their deformed hand and healing them.

He has such extraordinary presence and is so massively commanding and has so much authority that people who walk with Him marvel, saying, "He must be the Son of God." (See Matthew 16:16.)

A time lapse and everything goes dark for our next scene: a skinny man with a nervous look on his face followed by a band of soldiers are walking toward Jesus. The thin man kisses Jesus on the cheek—a betrayal with a kiss. We quickly realize that the guy is Judas, one of Jesus's disciples, come to betray him for a handful of silver.

The soldiers arrest Jesus, and it takes us to our next scene.

An interrogation room fills the screen, then time cuts: we see an angry soldier with a menacing look on his face lifting a whip.

This is hard to watch, and some of us look away or close our eyes in between glimpses. We see a whip with metal balls on the end being lifted and a Man with a bare back we recognize as Jesus; we look away and look back, and what we see is confusing—skin tearing, blood...a cry, then the scene changes.

It looks like the end of the movie, but we remember from our screenwriting class that there is something called a "false ending." It's not over yet!

The scene fades in on a tomb, and standing in front of the tomb, a Man looking very much like the King of kings and the Lord of lords. We hear the sound of a trumpet as His white garment whips in the wind!

Even after being killed, buried, spending three days and three nights in the pits of hell, and rising from the dead, Jesus is still bent on fulfilling purpose. It's still about telling people that the Kingdom of God is here, ready to impact and change this world! (See 1 Chronicles 29:11–12.)

The devil has tried but just can't keep this Guy down!

That scene is followed by a series of still shots: the shocked look on the face of the disciples as Jesus walks through the wall of a room and stands before them.

"Whoa!" says Peter, as he tries to get his mind around what just happened!

Next, the disciples sitting at the feet of Jesus as He commissions them to go into all the world and preach the gospel (see Mark 16:15), telling them not to be bashful, rather to use His Name (I feel the Holy Spirit's attention on this). And he tells them to expect the same power that was with Him to be with them! He promises them that a superpower called the Holy Spirit would come alongside them to help them (see John 14:15–17).

* * * * * * *

The disciples are about to learn that the Name, Jesus, is a big deal—a spiritual force that carries the same power as when Jesus walked the earth.

A pat on a drum, and another rapping chorus from some guys off camera as the scene changes to—

His disciples step into action!

> One day, Peter and John were going up to the temple…Now a man who was lame from birth was being carried to the temple gate called Beautiful, where he was put every day to beg…

Then Peter said, "Look at us!" So the man gave his attention expecting to get something from them.

Then Peter said, "Silver or gold I do not have, but what I do have I give you. In the name of Jesus Christ of Nazareth, walk." Taking him by the right hand, he helped him up, and instantly the man's feet and ankles became strong...He jumped to his feet...walking and jumping and praising God. (Acts 3:1–8, NIV)

The disciples are on "fire" as they go from town to town applying the name of Jesus to broken lives and bringing healing (I felt the Holy Spirit's attention on that).

As the lights go up in the theatre, we sit for a second trying to get our mind around what just happened—how the name of Jesus manages to be so radical and how it is a force that can reach into the life of a crippled man and cause him to walk! All that strength and power in a Name!

After the movie, we go to the Faith-Bridge Café, our imaginary on the page coffee and tea experience, to share what we experienced.

We see that the name of Jesus has no space/time limitations and is a spiritual force!

Jesus, by building a great name on earth as the Son of God and *the* Messiah, and by having courage to bear His great name (to not give up under pressure)—placed Himself in a powerful position!

He gained the respect of people who identified Him as one with superior name and character; so superior that even in His physical absence, they could apply His name to situations in their lives and experience the same miracles and transformations as when He walked the earth.

The name of Jesus, unlike Maximus Meridius, is not lengthy and elaborate, but it is keenly powerful! A name is only as powerful as its bearer; therefore, Jesus, being infinitely strong, bears a great name, indeed.

It took courage for Jesus to bear his great name, to wear it even when some people despised him and would have preferred for him to draw back and disappear into the shadows. He bore His name even when it meant going to the cross!

* * * * * * *

Jesus has a purpose-driven name. The great name He built was connected to His great purpose. In other words, it was necessary for Him to have a great name if He were to achieve such a great purpose, namely, the redemption of mankind.

Hidden in the name is the description of the purpose. The name Jesus, Yeshua in Hebrew, "is a form of the Hebrew verb yasha which means to deliver, save or rescue."[52]

The enormous resistance He experienced from His enemies was to convince Him to "kill His name," or abandon His purpose. By bearing His name, despite great pressure and by living up to the responsibility of His name, the world could now be saved—His purpose being fulfilled!

Salvation, as Jesus requires it, is based on the believer calling on His name! The rescue is in the name (I feel the Holy Spirit's attention on this). The name holds power! It is not just a word, it is *the* Word—the "spiritual force" through which all was made, and the "spiritual force" through which all will be redeemed.

Jesus came to destroy the works of the devil and save the lost. (See 1 John 3:8, and Luke 19:10.) His impeccable character and great name make salvation possible.

Jesus the Christ: He is God the Son.

* * * * * * *

Trailblazer, if you are born of God, you inherited a great name! And that name will attract some resistance! Some of you who have stepped out in Christian ministry are going through some wars that you don't tell anyone about because they wouldn't believe you! It's not that they are bad people, it's just that they may not be educated on the topic of spiritual warfare (or to your particular warfare), so some of what you are going through is unimaginable to them.

You know the spiritual attacks are real because you are living through it. The advances against you, against the very air you breathe, may be a deliberate attempt to de-rail your purpose, or "kill" your name. (I felt the Holy Spirit's attention on this.) It's because those born of God, those who trust in Jesus, have a great name, and have a great purpose—to share the gospel of Jesus, the Christ! To carry that name despite the "danger" or spiritual opposition requires great courage!

Jesus understands this challenge. He said "If you belonged to the world, it would love you as its own. As it is, you do not belong to the world, but I have chosen you out of the world. That is why the world hates you" (John 15:19, NIV).

Kingdom citizens that confess Jesus as their Lord experience this paradox—being in the world but not of it! They find that they must be stronger than others, more focused, and more courageous, and more is required of them than of others. It is all because we carry the name of Jesus, we identify with His name and His purpose, and we catch a bit of fire because of it. But it is our responsibility, having been born into the family of God and having inherited salvation through His great name, to own up to the challenges, to man up or woman up to it!

* * * * * * *

The reason Jesus is so attractive to millions of people is because He bears His name with such extreme courage, and because He has been so effective in presenting a name to humanity that has such fascinating far reaching results! His name, in a sense, is a cosmic force. It spans eternity. As it rolls through the universe it changes everything it touches, bringing peace and stability in a crazy world. Those who carry the name of Jesus, those who believe on His name, feel this thing that is so much greater than us!

As a Kingdom citizen, as one born of God, you have the Name. Don't be afraid to use it, but use it carefully.

46

Kingdom Privilege

Strength to Persevere

I checked the time on my cell phone and saw that I had an hour left to review my notes before heading out the door for my law school exam, scheduled to begin promptly at 11:00 a.m. I would get a cup of tea and try to relax my mind before taking the ten-minute drive to the school campus. I reasoned that I would arrive on campus with a good thirty minutes to spare.

At around 10:15 a.m., I got in my car and checked the digital clock on the dashboard. It read 11:15 a.m. I looked at it again, and again. Then, I dialed 411!

"Hello," a calm voice said on the other end. "This is…"

"What time is it?" I was breathless.

"Time?" the soft voice said back to me.

"Yes! The time. What is it?"

"Well, ma'am," she said, followed by a long pause, "it's 11:17 a.m."

My cell phone clock rolled back one hour? How is that possible? It's not daylight saving time. I hung up the phone and peeled out the driveway!

Around eight minutes later I pulled up to the school campus, found a parking spot and ran into the building and up a single flight of stairs. I slowly opened the door and saw the other students working hard at their exams. The teacher looked up at me then looked away in disgust. "May I speak to you?" I asked timidly.

I was standing in the doorway, waiting for his response. Professor Stark got up from his desk, his eyes looking at me as if I was a naughty two-year old, and waved me into the hallway. He was furious!

I blurted out a string of words and tried to explain what happened. "Well, that's just too bad!" he quipped. "I told everyone at the beginning of the semester that there would be no late starts to exams." I didn't remember him ever saying that, but it was no time to argue.

"If you would just let me pick up here and finish in the time left, I'd really appreciate it." I knew it was a long shot. I tried to maintain some semblance of self-control, resisting the borderline panic brewing in my mind!

The class was a nightmare for me from the start, and I had managed to keep steady grades despite the harsh atmosphere that whirled up each time Stark stepped into the room. He was not someone I wanted to irritate; but I knew that if I could take the final exam and get a grade of just fifty percent, I would still pass the course.

"Go sit in the hallway at the table!" he said and walked off without any explanation. He was referring to the sole table in the hallway, near the stairs and next to a window.

As I sat at the table, I wondered how I got into this mess. I looked out at the pine trees lining the far side of the driveway and thought about all I had gone through to get to my third year in the rigorous school program. This was one of two final exams left, and I needed to pass both of them to avoid jeopardizing my graduation, to avoid throwing away nights upon nights of studying and slaving over definitions, case briefs, and class notes.

A first-generation college student from a poor village in Jamaica, I sometimes felt like an imposter, as if I was living someone else's dream. I had no frame of reference, no one to tell me that I wasn't mad for doing this—for enrolling in one of the toughest academic programs in the country. Now it was all in jeopardy.

I watched the time drain away from me. By now, the rest of the class was getting into the second section of the exam. Fifteen minutes later, the teacher returned, still fuming! "Go to the dean's office," he commanded, "and if the dean says you can take the exam, I will let you take it."

He had hardly finished the sentence when I was already running down the stairs. I hurried into the administration office and stopped at the reception desk. "Dean Harvey, please, I need to talk to him!" The receptionist went over and knocked on his door. Less than a minute later, he was standing in front of me. I told him I was late to the exam and the teacher said I needed his permission to sit for it. He looked at me with pity in his eyes, as if saying, "Why are you standing in front of me? Why aren't you in the room taking the exam?" Finally, he said, "Go! Use the time that's left."

When I got back upstairs, I was numb. I felt exhausted. I quietly opened the classroom door. When the teacher walked over to me, I managed the words, "He said okay."

He picked up an exam from his desk and saw me back into the hallway. Then, he led me down a long adjacent hallway that ran the length of the building.

He found a small windowless room to the right with a single desk and chair and dropped the exam on the desk. "Leave your things on the chair outside the room," he commanded.

I looked into the hallway and saw a chair at the far end of the hall. I hurried over to it, rested my pocketbook on it, and went back to the room. I sat down behind the desk, with no way to check the time, as he closed the door and walked off. I had about forty-five minutes to take the two-hour exam.

I had to block out the thought of my purse, credit card, and other personal belongings sitting on a chair in the lonely hallway outside the door and focus on the exam. As it turned out, I failed the exam, but by the grace of God, earned a strong enough overall score to make 72 percent for the course. I thought the worst was over, but Professor Stark had other plans!

Before handing in our grades, he announced that he had decided to change the grading system, giving greater weight to the final exam, the one that I had failed. His new grading system effectively dropped my grade to 65 percent, which was unacceptable for my program.

As a woman of color, one of the few black faces at the college, I felt like a dinosaur, marked for extinction, and flagged for failure. I was among the small percentage of black women across the Country enrolled in law school, and I was determined! (I felt God's attention on that.) In any case, I couldn't afford another low grade. I had one exam left to take in another course, and this one would seal my fate; this one would determine whether I graduated or not.

On the night preceding my very last exam, I had two time pieces on the ready—my cell phone and a small clock as back up, just in case. On the morning of my exam, I checked my cell phone, and indeed, it had again mysteriously rolled back one hour giving the illusion that it was actually earlier than it was! But I had that second clock on standby, so this time, I arrived to the exam room with plenty of time to spare!

On graduation day, my mother and the rest of my family were beaming. We were a long way from the little shack in Jamaica with the leaky zinc roof that our family had called home for so many years.

They had no idea the many challenges I faced to get to that moment, we were just glad that I made it! (I felt God's attention on that.) And how I thank God for strengthening me, for listening to my prayers about my exams, and for seeing me to that day! (I felt the Holy Spirit's attention on that.)

Law school school taught me about staying calm in conflict and thinking things through, and I had really good teachers. I wouldn't trade that experience. I've learned that adversity, as stunning and uncomfortable as it feels at the time, is not an enemy; it can be useful. God allowed me to have the experience (I felt the Holy Spirit's attention on that) because it would teach me to persevere.

In keeping, Professor Stark was not my enemy. Deliberate or not, his harsh tactics throughout the semester made me stronger.

Years later, and I still can't explain the mystery of the cell phone clock rolling back an hour (twice) during finals; nevertheless, I needed to handle the consequences, and with God's help (I felt God's attention on that), I prevailed.

* * * * * * *

Kingdom positioning has incredible relevance! It is a smart move for anyone who wants to partner with an eternal Empire; a fantastic and powerful community that is very real and very significant! So I am learning that it resembles law school in the fact that it doesn't shield me from adversity (I felt the Holy Spirit's attention on that).

God warns me when there is a storm coming, but He allows me to go through it because there is something in the experience that is valuable to me. The storms make me stronger, teaches me to *persevere*, and to rely on God. As it says in scripture:

> Consider it pure joy, my brothers and sisters, whenever you face trials of many kinds. Because you know that the testing of your faith produces perseverance. Let perseverance finish its work so that you may be mature and complete, not lacking anything. If any of you lacks wisdom, you should ask God, who gives generously to all without finding fault, and it will be given to you. (James 1:2–4, NIV)

The stories in this book span decades, and hopefully you noticed the faithfulness of God unfolding on the pages! Notice too that by the loving grace of God, I have grown (I felt the Holy Spirit's attention on this) in faith. I say this only to prove that if you stay the course, if you persevere and don't give up when life gets tough, your relationship with God *will* get stronger, you *will* mature (I felt the

Holy Spirit's attention on this) and what used to trip you up will be ineffective some time from now.

The adversity you bump into along the way will build your faith muscles and make you a stronger person; but you have to be determined to persevere, to finish what you start! Trust God and He will help you, and His heart is gracious and kind.

I am the evidence.

47

Kingdom Duty

Turn and Strengthen

I parked my car in front of a huge brick building and walked along a side street to the front entrance. This particular brick building, sitting near quaint old houses that whaling captains once lived in, is a massive structure enclosed by high walls topped off with chards of glass and barbed wire; or at least that's how I remember it now.

I slowed my pace as I approached the building, then stepped inside a narrow doorway leading to a security booth. I must have given my identification to the guard at the door, but I don't remember. He must have gone over a set of rules for visitors to the prison, but I don't remember that either. Life fell into slow motion when I lifted my eyes and saw the monster in the room—a massive cage-wall that ran from floor to ceiling!

The blood must have drained from my face as I tried to get my mind around the structure looming in front of me! It was brown and thick and went at least two stories high. It was a cage. A cage for humans. I didn't understand it! *A cage? They put my brother in a cage?*

Finally, I heard a voice, a male voice say, "Go up to the wall and sit down on the bench." The bench? I noticed it for the first time.

The voice belonged to the security guard at the door—a white man in a blue uniform. I managed to turn and look in his direction.

I saw sympathy in his eyes—his eyes asking me questions I couldn't answer.

"What are you doing here? How did you get to the point where you walked into a place like this?" I could see it in his eyes, but he wouldn't speak it.

"I don't know." I wanted to tell him. "My brother is here." I wanted to tell him that my brother didn't belong here. That he was really a good kid who got mixed up with drugs. But instead, I told my feet to move toward the cage and sit on that brown bench next to the wall.

And I sat there watching young men and fathers and grandfathers walk up and down the stairs. Then, I heard my brother's voice reaching through the bars—a timid, frightened voice from the other side.

I'm an unknown writer in a little town near Cape Cod, a beachy spot on the East Coast. But I think as long as a few people might read this book, it might be worthwhile to protest (I feel God's attention on this) the injustices happening to our young black and Latino youth in America (and around the world.)

According to a 2013 article, "While people of color make up 30 percent of the United States' population, they account for 60 percent of those imprisoned. The prison population grew by 700 percent from 1970 to 2005...1 in every 15 African American men and 1 in every 36 Hispanic men are incarcerated in comparison to 1 in every 106 white men."[53]

How are we, the church, responding and dealing with youth crimes in our community? Are we relying on the prisons to rehabilitate our youth, when we should be relying on God? (I felt God's attention on this.) Are we going to God for strategies of early intervention?

And how is the prison system shaping the identity of our youth? Can we, as a church, do better? (I felt God's attention on this.)

This is not an argument against correction; this is an argument for church intervention. (I felt the Holy Spirit's attention on this.)

I'm sorry the church is silent on this issue, at least many are (I feel God's attention on this). I'm pointing a finger at myself as well (I felt God's attention on that); because I too have been complacent at times.

This chapter is not an effort to be soft on crime. This is a plea for more early church-based/community-wide intervention so that minority youth incarceration doesn't continue to develop as a pandemic. We have the name of Jesus and the power of the Holy Spirit (I felt the Holy Spirit on that) to turn this around.

* * * * * * *

If you are reading this today, and you or someone you know is incarcerated, don't give up hope. Guilty or not, for those who repent and turn to God, He has a plan of redemption, forgiveness and restoration. This chapter is an invitation to step out of a crime lifestyle, to realize that it doesn't have to define your future (I felt the Holy Spirit's attention on that). God is merciful and a Master at restoring shattered lives!

God has promised: "…Believe on the Lord Jesus Christ, and you will be saved—you and your household" (Acts 16:31, NIV).

As Jesus says in the Bible, "Behold, I stand at the door and knock. If anyone hears My voice and opens the door, I will come in to him and dine with him, and he with Me" (Revelations 3:20, NKJV).

If you are incarcerated, remember God has a plan for your life. It begins with accepting Jesus as Lord and Savior. Take a step of faith and say this life-changing prayer from the Billy Graham Evangelistic Association.

Prayer of Salvation

"Dear Lord Jesus, I know I am a sinner, and I ask for your forgiveness. I believe you died for my sins and rose from the dead. I trust and follow you as my Lord and Savior. Guide my life and help me to do your will. In your name, amen."[54]

And when you are strengthened, turn and strengthen your brothers (see Luke 22:32).

48

Kingdom Duty

Listen

One day while I was driving to work, I had a strong impression to switch lanes and drive behind a truck. I felt it was a word from the Lord, but it didn't make sense. Trucks kick up gravel. I've had more than one pebble ricochet off my windshield from truck tires, and trucks are slow.

I wanted to keep moving, but after a few seconds of deliberation, I succumbed and fell back behind the truck. *Okay, Lord. This doesn't make sense to me, but I'll do it!* Then, seconds later, two vehicles crashed in the lane next to mine and went off road! The lane I had been traveling in was a danger zone! By "listening" and obeying the voice of God, I was at a safe distance, shielded by the truck.

On another occasion, I was driving in my hometown to a local bakery. I was seconds away when I had a sudden urge in my spirit to turn around and visit the animals at the local shelter, which was a few blocks away. It was so strong that I complied, and minutes later, I was sitting in front of the animal shelter. Suddenly, I remembered my allergy to cats and chose not to go in but stayed in my car and drove to the bakery.

I parked my car at the side of the building and walked through the doors in time to hear the owner of the bakery speaking on the phone. He said, "Hello, police. We have just been robbed!" I missed a robbery by seconds! If I hadn't obeyed that urge to take that little detour to the animal shelter, I would have walked into a robbery in progress! By the grace of God, I was a few blocks away at a safe distance when it happened!

If I was resistant or "stiff necked" in both those case, I might have gotten seriously injured. (I felt the Holy Spirit's attention on that.)

I don't always get it right, but I am learning that it is always wise to listen up when God speaks, and to comply quickly! Here is an example from scripture that shows how God values those who listen and heed His warnings:

> The Word which came to Jeremiah from the Lord...saying, "Go to the house of the Rechabites, speak to them, and bring them into the house of the Lord, into one of the chambers, and give them wine to drink."
>
> But they said, "We will drink no wine, for Jonadab the son of Rechabab, our father, commanded us, saying, 'You shall drink no wine, you nor your sons, forever...' Thus we have obeyed..."
>
> Then came the word of the Lord to Jeremiah, saying, "Thus says the Lord of hosts, the God of Israel: 'Go and tell the men of Judah and the inhabitants of Jerusalem, "Will you not receive instruction to obey My words?"'" says the Lord.
>
> "The words of Jonadab the son of Rechabab, which he commanded his sons, not to drink wine, are performed; for to this day they drink none and obey their father's commandment. But although I have spoken to you, rising early and speaking, you did not obey Me."

And Jeremiah said to the house of the Rechabites, "Thus says the Lord of hosts, the God of Israel: 'Because you have obeyed the commandment of Jonadab your father...Rechabab shall not lack a man to stand before Me forever.'" (Jeremiah 35:1–19, NKJV)

In the story, Jonadab warned his sons not to drink wine to protect them, perhaps to keep them mobile and alert in a hostile land.

Just as Jonadab was trying to save his sons from trouble by giving them instructions that would prolong their lives, so too God has our survival in mind. He speaks to save lives, and so listening is imperative. The house of the Rechabites understood this—the importance of listening when a father speaks—they valued the voice of their father.

So, too, God gives lifesaving instructions to the citizens of His Kingdom, the obedience of which brings safety while disobedience opens the door to a storm.

The storm is simply a ship-wrecking life without God's instructions and guidance.

God rewards those who value *His* voice—the voice of our heavenly Father! He has incredible perspective, and when He gives instructions, it's always wise to say, "Yes, Lord."

So I am learning that the amount of safety in the life of a Kingdom citizen is directly proportional to how well the citizen listens to the Voice of God and heeds instruction.

49

Kingdom Duty

Loyalty

I was hesitant to include this next chapter because I felt the message should come from someone else, maybe a pastor of a church, not me; but in the end, I felt it should be included. (I felt the Holy Spirit's attention on that.)

As I laid sleeping in my apartment in the Mojave Desert, I had a dream. This is a bit of a riddle, as most dreams are. This dream seems to carry a relevant message that affects us all. I share the main parts of it here:

> In the dream, I saw a place that looked like a nightclub. People were seated at tables, socializing and chatting.
>
> There was a dark-skinned man with a smooth complexion behind the bar, who I will refer to as the "Bartender." Then I saw a female celebrity sitting near the Bartender...
>
> The celebrity was a particular famous singer in earlier decades, like the eighties, but had not had a hit for years, and she was eager for attention.

Next, I saw the celebrity wearing a gold bodysuit and walking up and down the night-club isle, along with a backup singer, singing for the crowd who were wowed by her "pop music."

Then, suddenly, the night club turned into a church building and the same crowd from the nightclub was now in a church service. The transition from nightclub to church was virtually seamless. The celebrity was now a star feature in the church and the church members were mesmerized by the celebrity's music.

The entire congregation joined her in singing a type of worship music. The song was wrapped in a sweet melody and the church sang it unto God in unison. They sang, "With the lies of Jesus, what's become of Him?" In other words, the devil was leading worship!

As the church members worshipped inside the church, I saw a woman standing in the church lobby taking pictures of herself with her camera phone. She was unconcerned, or perhaps unaware, about what was going on inside the church sanctuary and was infatuated with her own appearance.

Then I woke.

As I woke, still very much half asleep, the song was still playing in my mind, and it seemed rather pleasant until I, more awake now, started to examine the words of the song: "With the lies of Jesus, what's become of Him?" Then, I understood that the celebrity in the dream and the message in the song were anti-Christ—the devil was the worship leader—and I understood that tragically, the church represented in the dream had been deceived into thinking that their music was true and acceptable worship unto God.

The church had in fact morphed into an institution of idolatry.

This is my spin on the dream:

First, the Bartender represents the devil and demons—in this case, a demonic spirit of intoxication—a wooing and lulling spirit, sent to the church with the assignment of providing intoxicants or diversions.

The Bartender starts slowly and gradually introduces higher degrees of intoxicants. In other worlds, he takes territory gradually. He begins by introducing a diversion to the church body that often takes the form of a popular individual, such as a celebrity singer, but it could be any influential individual.

As the church embraces the celebrity, the Bartender is then able to use the charisma and soothing "music" of the celebrity to deliver a "hidden" anti-Christ message. To deliver a curse. His goal is to hijack the pulpit and transform the congregation.

So for example, as seen in the dream, step one of the Bartender's approach is to find a celebrity (any influential individual, someone who is a hybrid—meaning that he or she is committed in their heart to the "world" but also "performs" in the church).

Next, the Bartender finds a church without a God-committed pastor and convinces him or her to give the celebrity the pulpit.

Once the Bartender has accomplished that, it's just a matter of time before the church changes course and becomes anti-Christ.

In the dream, the Bartender uses a popular singer, but I think the point is that the Bartender can use any "celebrity"—popular performer, businessman, athlete, politician, wealthy old woman, etc.—to carry out his devices. The Bartender's goal is to find someone anti-Christ and get him or her to the pulpit, to the *center* of attention!

Of course, there are some "celebrities," rich people, and popular musicians, etc. in the church that are sincere and devoted to God and are a blessing to the congregation; but the celebrity used by the Bartender is Christian on the outside only.

If the pastor aligns his thinking with the Bartender and welcomes the celebrity, then the pastor will ignore the fact that the celebrity cares nothing about Jesus and will integrate the celebrity into the most sacred positions in the church, like singing and leading worship, precisely what the devil wanted.

The payoff for the demon-hearted celebrity is attention, receiving the worship of the congregation and gaining a following (winning a Christian audience to their detriment).

The payoff for the Bartender is getting full control of the pulpit and the congregation and shipwrecking that church's destiny.

The payoff for the pastor is that he gains new members to his congregation and even megachurch status (I felt the Holy Spirit's attention on that), and in some cases, hefty financial backing, and in most cases, a large ego as his congregation swells to large numbers.

The reward for all who participate is total and complete spiritual bankruptcy (I felt God's attention on this).

Once the celebrity is introduced into the fabric of the church, the pastor, who has experienced financial backing and popularity (and has effectively "sold out" by being disloyal and abandoning his obligation to God and the congregation) begins to feel continually obligated to the celebrity. The pastor, who now is in service to the celebrity, becomes irrational (more intoxicated) and does things like having the celebrity lead church worship and take the reins of the church.

The celebrity, motivated by a demonic spirit of lies, uses hybridized worship songs to deceive the congregation.

In other words, the song has two layers. One layer is superficial and includes the words being mouthed by the celebrity, and to the ear of an untrained listener, sounds like perfectly fine "worship" music that praises and worships God.

But there is a second layer—the song holds a curse! There is an anti-Christ "energy and bad vibe," a demonic influence emanating from the heart of the celebrity and infecting the message with underlying layers of unbelief. There is no faith to the music, just hidden corruption. More specifically, there is a deadly current of unbelief hidden between each note of the music. The unbelieving celebrity can only give what he or she has to give from the heart—unbelief and a hidden anti-Christ message!

In other words, the celebrity who knowingly or unknowingly hates Jesus emanates corruption, defilement, curses, and death in the fabric of the music. It's in the tone of her voice and emanates from her (or his) soul. It is a spiritual attack on the church and the death assignment of the music must be spiritually discerned.

The celebrity's assignment is to derail the congregation, to get it off track, to crash it! It is a calculated strategy by the devil, the father of lies. "He was a murderer from the beginning, not holding to the truth, for there is no truth in him. When he speaks he speaks his native language for he is a liar" (John 8:44, NIV). The scripture says when the devil speaks, he speaks lies, and perhaps the same can be said when he sings. When he sings, he sings (injects) lies.

The tactic of the Bartender and the celebrity could result in the fall of a church if the pastor allows the invasion. In the dream, the church did fall. (I am referring here to an individual church and not the Church at large.)

In the entire dream, there was no pastor on the scene, or at least he could not be identified. He was absent spiritually, if not physically. He was not fulfilling his role as pastor, and the congregation was left without a covering.

The saddest part of the dream is that the entire congregation, being led by the celebrity, and covertly by the Bartender, sincerely sang to God in worship.

The congregation was totally convinced that they were worshiping God. They were quite sincere when they sang the words against Jesus, but they had no idea that they were completely deceived. They were not supporters of Jesus. The words they sang, if they listened with spiritual ears, very much opposed the Messiah.

They let the Bartender get control of their pulpit and the world and they became one—one voice, one heart, and one anti-Christ spirit. No one in the church protested because it all happened with the sleight of hand and because they were too busy enjoying themselves to notice. Little baby compromises led to a big mess.

The celebrity performer was dangerous in the pulpit because her heart wasn't consecrated to God and she had the heart (worshiped the god) of this world. She had her own master, apart from God. The members/leadership of the church failed to recognize this and failed to guard the "doors "of the church sanctuary. That led to their fall, but it wasn't a messy, obvious fall. They were totally ignorant of their condition. Eventually, they blended with the infiltrator to such an extent that they could no longer be identified as separate.

Notice too that the celebrity in the dream was wearing a "gold" bodysuit. It's all about the money!! Sadly, the pastor and the congregation in the dream may have been tempted to ignore the darkness eminating from the celebrity in exchange for a hefty payoff each Sunday (I see the devil's attention on that); if the church is flourishing financially and growing rapidly. It's big business (I see the devil's attention on that). If money is pouring in from the celebrity-influence, the leadership may be willing to close their eyes to the effects (I sense God's attention on that.)

Some churches, if given the chance, may welcome the opportunity to be financially lucritive, at the cost of true worship. They may close their eyes to the fact that something perverse has hijacked the worship service because of all the luxary it affords them.

Finally, the woman in the dream taking pictures of herself with her camera phone is a testimony of vanity that dominates the minds of some women (and men) in the church. Women are often the gate keepers of the church, and it was no mistake that even though she stood in the lobby next to the church entrance that she paid no attention to what was going on around her. She didn't notice who was coming through those church doors, and she didn't seem to care. Her only concern was her makeup, hair, and clothes.

She was caught up in idolatry. She failed in her responsibility to watch the door, to see who was infiltrating the church, to be alert and prayerful because she was busy taking selfies and totally consumed by her appearance. She was dominated by a spirit of vanity and failed in her role as a mother and overseer in the church.

While she was busy taking pictures of her perfectly coifed hair and admiring her makeup, the people in the church pews were sinking. They were being lied to and literally dying.

As women in the Church, we must be careful and remember to keep God as our main motive and focus. It's not about who we can impress but Who we can impress. We can impress God by being gatekeepers, for example. Instead of being in the lady's room during worship fixing our hair and makeup (I'm guilty of this), we could arrive early to do that, so that we can be in the sanctuary praying for the service before it begins, and ask God to block dark demonic spirits that might try to infiltrate the service. We can function as extraordinary gatekeepers and can help prevent our church from sinking by interceding before God!

If we (all members, not just women) fail God in this, an incredible loss could follow such neglect!

In the end, it is a test of loyalty to God. Are we being swept up by pop culture and a tolerance of idols? Have we fallen into idolatry, one church at a time? Is it about the beat, the tempo, the loudness of the music and songs, the "rock concert atmosphere," or is it about humility and consecration to God? (I felt the Holy Spirit's attention on this.)

As individuals who profess Jesus as Lord, if God were to search our hearts, would he find us loyal to His Kingdom or self-deceived and filled with idolatry?

Test our hearts, Lord, and let the examination start with me. My prayer is that we not only recognize the problem but that we do something about it!

50

Kingdom Privilege

Independence

S unlight is flickering through mango and banana trees and bouncing off the dirt path in front of me as I make my way through the bush to an old shack in the Jamaican hills. An aroma of chicken with gravy fills the air and seems to wrap around me as I walk up to the door and wait. In the back of my mind is my grandfather's warning never to beg the neighbors for food. But this isn't begging. This is standing by the door and waiting.

My heart is pounding as I wait for the old woman of the house to notice me. I know she is in there, cooking. So I wait silently. The ground feels cool under my bare, dusty feet, as I stand there watching the empty doorway. Waiting.

Finally, the old woman appears at the door, gives me a tired glance, and walks away. A few minutes later, she returns with a bowl of food, leans over, hands it to me, then walks away without saying a word.

I eat quickly then scurry off toward the bush.

Light is pilfering through the mango and banana trees, and there is a cool breeze coming up from the river.

* * * * * * *

313

Many years later and I still remember what it felt like to be a child (around six years old) and not have enough to eat—watching the same story unfold each evening—Mama trying to get enough food on the plate. Sometimes, dinner would be a very small meal, maybe a few dumplings. That's how I ended up walking through the bush to a neighbor's house and standing at their door at dinnertime. And sometimes, the neighbors' children would end up standing at our door, and Mama would find a way to feed them.

Fortunately, a lot has changed for my family since those meager years in Jamaica, with many moving off the island to etch out a better life elsewhere. But this story is not so much about me as it is a tribute to those who still struggle in poverty, their little houses dotting the hillside, those families who still worry about feeding their children.

* * * * * * *

Having had a firsthand experience with poverty on the island, I felt a lot of emotions when I came across a 2011 article[55] in the Jamaican Gleaner titled, "Give Us the Queen."

According to the Gleaner,[56] the word on the street is that many Jamaicans are desperate for a change. It says that 60 percent of Jamaicans surveyed would consider being reconciled to Great Britain, their former colonizer, after losing heart in the grips of poverty, substandard education and violence.

They want a better future for their children, and they want to swallow their pride and take the hand of a superpower nation that can help them get up from the mess. So some Jamaicans look longingly toward the British Empire hoping for reconciliation, leadership, an opportunity to "bounce" back and to steady economically and socially.

The nineteenth and twentieth century history of Jamaica-Britain relationship was volatile and British rule was sometimes tyrannical. So perhaps at least in 1962 and prior, Jamaica's fight for independence made sense. However, the 2011 article[57] in the Gleaner reported that many Jamaicans believe they would be better off if Jamaica had remained a British colony. The article seems to allude to the fact that Britain, despite its own problems, would be a huge stabilizing force for the tiny island nation.

That brings us to the topic at hand. When is independence a bad idea? Perhaps the answer is: when it's not working, when people are worse off because of it. That, in effect, is what some Jamaicans are saying. This independence thing isn't working as well as we had hoped.

So what options do we have?

The Empire of the Kingdom of God. As established earlier, The Kingdom of God is an eternal spiritual Kingdom under the rule and Kingship of the God of Abraham. (See Psalm 45:6.) It exists in the spirt realm but is very real, more real and more relevant than this physical realm.

At some point the entire earth was under the dominion and control of the Kingdom of God. Then, God created man and woman and gave them dominion over the earth. But Adam and Eve being influenced by the outlaw-deceiver satan, got the idea to revolt against God's commands, and so God gave them their independence. (See Genesis 3.) Adam and Eve were then left to choose for themselves and make their own way.

What resulted was the opposite of what Adam and Eve had imagined and the opposite of what the devil had promised. While the Kingdom of God went on to be the most stable, wealthy and influential superpower, the newly independent Adam and Eve (and their descendants) began a journey of intense and painful struggle and decline. (See Genesis 3:17.)

Thereafter, earth and its people spiraled downward, suffering famines, wars, and insane acts of genocide. Some would argue that this is all a result of people's insistence on independence from the Kingdom of God and the ways of God. By rejecting God, people's positioning changed. They no longer came under His dominion or His covering. He still aided where He could, but the privileges people could access would not be near the level it would have been had they remained under His Kingdom rule.

Several people, apart from the larger masses, have been re-annexed to the Kingdom of God, through Jesus, the Son of God (see

Romans 5:8 and John 3:16–17). We have been engrafted back into the Kingdom. This occurs through a born-again experience, through the rejuvenating power of the Holy Spirit (see John 3:5).

The new birth makes us legitimate citizens of the Kingdom of God and His Empire (see Philippians 3:20). This is a critically important positioning because we come under the dominion of a spiritual Kingdom that avails us enormous covering and opportunity.

We make a decision to return to God and His Kingdom because independence isn't working and more importantly, because He loves us (see John 3:16).

What the world offers is rather pathetic and spiritually bankrupt in comparison to what God lavishes on us as citizens of His Kingdom—eternal life, healing, wholeness, a Jeremiah 29:11 blessing. So in the Kingdom of God, dependence brings independence. It brings all the qualities you would expect in a State of Independence—livelihood, freedom from evil oppressive rule, national security, and healthy life.

Apart from God and His Kingdom, we are left to our devices—our own strength and decision making. One glance at a television newscast very much sums up the result of independence from God.

On a planetary level, we see a world separated from the Kingdom of God by rebellion and this insistence on independence, resulting in a world that tolerates aborting children in the womb, child trafficking, poverty, and unimaginable violence! It seems obvious that we need the Kingdom of God! We need that Superpower to come alongside and bring stability, mercifully restore our shattered lives, bring forgiveness, peace, and reconstruct a future that will bless all children.

Since we have choices in life, at what point do we say, "our independence isn't working," and choose a system that does work? Corporations get this. They merge all the time for the sake of what they can accomplish together, the lesser corporation benefiting from the strength of the greater; but in the end, both will benefit. An unwise corporation in trouble would resist partnership, insisting on ruling by themselves and continuing in their old ways, until they eventually tank.

It's smart to return to the Kingdom of God, to acknowledge the enormous benefits of His relationship, of His governance. Unlike a man-led monarchy, we don't have to be concerned about greed, hidden agendas, or corruption in His Kingdom.

I won't claim to know everything there is to know about the Kingdom of God. Having said that, I know enough to realize that in my personal life, positioning myself in the Kingdom of God has saved my life!

I tell about escaping danger in the first chapter of this book. God rescued me from the hands of kidnappers! I believe God was able to intervene, send angels if you will, because I am a citizen of His Kingdom.

More importantly, I have been saved from a life apart from God—my salvation, my citizenship is eternal. A life apart from God is a song that sounds like the cries in a Holocaust. It is dark and dismal. In the Kingdom, there is life and life abundantly.

The point is, we have an attractive answer to our personal and world struggles, to our messy independence. We are smart to return to God. The Kingdom of God is about lifting the masses, about bringing restoration! That's the entire gospel of Jesus Christ. The whole purpose behind His life in the earth was to announce the Kingdom of God is at hand—to engraft those who would become citizens, to provide a better future, to give eternal life (see John 10:10 and Matthew 4:17).

The Kingdom of God extends citizenship to individuals, and individuals who are frustrated by the present world's way of doing things can decide to return to the Kingdom. We don't have to wait for a political assembly to give us permission.

Regardless of what the masses decide, anyone who has the heart to do so can sculpt a victory by being reconciled to God and His kingdom through Jesus as Lord. Jesus presents an incredible window back into the Kingdom, an enormous opportunity for partnership with God! As we enter in, God will go about bringing stability. For His plans for those who return to His Kingdom are good, not evil, to give us a future and a hope (see Jeremiah 29:11).

Jamaica is proud of its independence won by men and women with brave hearts, like my great-great-grandfather, Paul Bogle, the Jamaican national hero. This chapter that questions independence is not to discredit their efforts, or the efforts of the many strong and dedicated leaders that have followed them, but to merely present the question of effectiveness *after* independence. And so, the question is not just about Jamaica, but this global issue of decline; if not financially, then too often, spiritually.

So then we are left with the question: "What will we do in response?"

Fortunately, we have free will, as individuals, to make decisions that re-align us with the Kingdom of God, and consequently, a better future. For those of us who choose that path, we realize the value of surrendering our lives to God. (I felt the Holy Spirit's attention on that.)

God's Kingdom provides eternal life, and in this present world, safety and provision (see Philippians 4:19 and John 3:16). But this will require Kingdom of God alignment, and this alignment brings independence from oppression and decline.

Returning to God as King, returning to His Kingdom rule is the key to a safe and prosperous future! Returning to Kingdom rule starts with saying "Yes" to Jesus.

Here is another opportunity for you to know Jesus as Lord, to enter the Kingdom of God. Say this simple prayer from the Billy Graham Evangelistic Association:

Prayer of Salvation

"Dear Lord Jesus, I know I am a sinner, and I ask for your forgiveness. I believe you died for my sins and rose from the dead. I trust and follow you as my Lord and Savior. Guide my life and help me to do your will. In your name, amen."[58]

Whatever you're going through, don't give up hope. There is a Kingdom and a God who cares. Choose reconciliation. His plans for you are good—to give you a future and amazing hope (see Jeremiah 29:11).

Jesus says, "I stand at the door and knock" (Revelation 3:20, NIV).

Time is short.

What will you decide?

Be courageous!

51

Courageous

So much of this book has been about God teaching me to be courageous. In the introduction, I told of how He sent an angel to encourage me right before I was about to begin my first professional job. I was young and insecure and really didn't know if I had it in me to take on the responsibilities of the new role. "Courageous," He said.

Fast forward several years later, and I have taken a lot of roads since then, one in particular that landed me at this computer talking to you through these pages—pages which I pray have inspired you to trust in Him in the hardest of times, in those painful moments.

As I sit here typing this, I feel a bit overwhelmed. I think this is my greatest test yet—the strongest demand for courage. I, like many of you, have been watching the news as the COVID-19 pandemic ceases humanity. I have also been watching the symptoms in my own body: the tightness in my chest, the trouble breathing and shortness of breath while speaking and walking, the weird feeling in my lungs, and the body chills.

And I have also been watching God (it's perhaps His greatest moment as well) to see how Heaven responds to my personal and world crisis. I still feel the presence of the Holy Spirit, and I feel a special urgency to finish this book.

I still get visions when I lay down at night of how I should respond, what might help my body to stay strong. And I watch my body, this vessel that has been so faithful to me, push back at something that I don't fully understand—push back at the symptoms, recover, relapse, recover, relapse, until I am sitting here wondering how this will end.

So as I laid awake around four this morning, I reconciled with death. I don't know how this will end, but I have this assurance in Him. I at least know that I have a connection, that I met Someone on this journey, and that He has blessed me. He stayed with me in the hot, unfriendly Mojave Desert in California and encouraged my heart; His was the voice that flowed in on the desert breeze. And He has been with me on all the other parts of this journey. His words have always been filled with faith of what I might become.

Maybe I will be seeing my Lord and Savior and maybe soon. That's how I feel at four in the morning when I lay awake staring up at the ceiling, in that secret place, in my own thoughts. Being here in this moment in time makes me feel for those suffering. I understand what they must be feeling, what it must be like to have foreign elements wreak havoc in one's body and mind. And I pray for us all.

Yet, as I laid awake this morning, I felt especially grateful for my relationship with God. I am happy that I took time to get to know Him, and I feel satisfied that if I were to take my last breath that I have this connection to His Kingdom.

Now, as I sit typing this, I feel the Holy Spirit prompting me to look up at my vision board! And so, I glance up at the six unmanifested dreams. There, to my left, is the one of my dreamhouse by the sea with the pine floors and sunny windows. I see too the dream I have about family, about getting married. I have other things on my vision board as well—words of inspiration. My eyes land on the words, "All is well" and "Fear not." And I sense God's kind attention. His presence is comforting to me.

I dry my eyes and take a deep breath.

Courage is doing what is hard or difficult when life is pressing in. God has been teaching me to be courageous.

Dear reader, *courageous*—that's His word to you too.

* * * * * *

Therefore, since we are receiving a kingdom that cannot be shaken, let us be thankful, and so worship God acceptably with reverence and awe. (Hebrews 12:28, NIV)

Endnotes

———

1   Merriam-Webster; https://merriam-Webster.com/dictionary/courage, accessed 1/10/16
2   Billy Graham Evangelistic Association, "Begin Your Journey to Peace." https://peacewithGod.net, Accessed 9/22/18.
3   Not actual name.
4   Not actual name.
5   Not actual name.
6   Billy Graham Evangelistic Association, https://cliffbarrowsmemorial.org/peacewithGod, accessed 8/2/20
7   Equiano Olaudah, *The Interesting Narrative of the Life of Olaudah Equiano, Written by Himself.* Edited by Robert J. Allison. New York. W. Durell, 1971. Reprint, Boston, Bedford Books 1995. (document w/o page numbers.)
8   Ibid.
9   Ibid.
10 CNN Breaking News, http://transcripts.cnn.com/TRANSCRIPTS/0109/11/bn.01.html
11 One Church International, 8pm service, Wednesday, November 12, 2014.
12 Ibid.
13 Ibid.
14 Ibid.
15 Ibid.
16 Billy Graham Evangelistic Association, https://cliffbarrowsmemorial.org/peacewithGod, accessed 8/2/20
17 https://en.m.wikipedia.org/wiki/Western_Wall, accessed 11/24/19
18 Billy Graham Evangelistic Association, https://cliffbarrowsmemorial.org/peacewithGod, accessed 8/2/20
19 https://m.youtube.com/watch?v=0FHyO6dniRC, accessed 6/9/19.
20 Ibid.
21 Ibid.
22 Ibid.
23 Ibid.
24 Ibid.

[25] Billy Graham Evangelistic Association, https://cliffbarrowsmemorial.org/peace-withGod, accessed 8/2/20

[26] https://www.lexico.com/en/definition/kingdom, accessed 7/2020

[27] https://www.britannica.com/place/United-Kingdom Accessed 10/20/18

[28] Ibid.

[29] https://www.thoughtco.com/constitutional-monarchy-fefinition-examples-4582648, accessed May 27, 2019.

[30] https://www.definitions.net/definition/absolute+monarchy (accessed 2/10/20)

[31] https://www.merriam-webster.com/dictionary/capital. Accessed 10/20/18

[32] Dr. Myles Munroe, *Kingdom Principles, Preparing for Kingdom Experience and Expansion,* Destiny Image Publishers, Inc. Shippensburg, PA., pg. 18–19, accessed 6/24/19.

[33] https://www.merriam-webster.com/dictionary/knowledge. Accessed 10/25/18

[34] Billy Graham Evangelistic Association, https://cliffbarrowsmemorial.org/peace-withGod, accessed 8/2/20

[35] Ibid.

[36] https://www.en.mwikipedia.org/wiki/Heathcare_in_England, accessed 5/5/20.

[37] https://www. gov.uk/working-abroad, accessed 5/5/20

[38] https://www.Etiavisa.com/etias-news/british-tourists-visiting-europe, accessed 5/5/20

[39] www.the-highway.com/genesis_Sproul.html. Accessed 11/26/14

[40] www.the-highway.com/genesis_Sproul.html. Accessed 11/26/14, and www.intouch.org/magazine/content.aspx?topic=The_New_Birth_and_Baptism_devotional#.VHeYWYrTnfo. Accessed 11/27/14.

[41] www.billwinston.org/bwm_newsDetail.aspx?id=399

[42] See Acts 2:4

[43] https://www.livestrong.com/article/450657-tamarind-for-diabetes/, accessed 7/27/19

[44] https://www.medicalnewstoday.com/articles/270435.php. Accessed 7/27/19

[45] https://www.diabetes-warrior.net/2011/04/08/liver-natures-vitamin -pill, accessed 7/27/19

[46] Billy Graham Evangelistic Association, https://cliffbarrowsmemorial.org/peace-withGod, accessed 8/2/20

[47] See 1 Samuel 16, Holy Bible

[48] See Luke 1:32, and see also https://biblehub.com/commentaries/jeremiah/33-17.htm, presenting Gil's Exposition of the Entire Bible/Jeremiah 33:17. Accessed 9/15/18.

[49] Cinderella, Walt Disney Productions, 1950. See also https: //en.m.wikipedia.org/wiki/Cinderella_(1950_film)

[50] Not her actual name, and the facts of the story may have been somewhat different than recollected here.

[51] The Lion King, Animated, Walt Disney Pictures, produced by Don Hahn, 1994.

[52] Hebrew Streams, The Hebrew Meaning of "Jesus," www.hebrew-streams.org/frontstuff//Jesus-Yeshua.html

[53] Kerby, Sophia. "The Top 10 Most Startling Facts About People of Color and Criminal Justice in the United States," https://www.americanprogress.org/issues/rce/news/2012/03/13/11351/the-top-10-most-startling-facts-about-people-of-color-and-criminal-justice-in-the-United-States/, Accessed October 10, 2018.

[54] Billy Graham Evangelistic Association, https://cliffbarrowsmemorial.org/peace-withGod, accessed 8/2/20

[55] "Give Us the Queen," The Gleaner, published June 28, 2011.

[56] Ibid.

[57] Ibid.

[58] Billy Graham Evangelistic Association, https://cliffbarrowsmemorial.org/peace-withGod, accessed 8/2/20

Bibliography

Equiano, Olaudah, *The Interesting Narrative of the Life of Olaudah Equiano, Written by Himself.* Edited by Robert J. Allison. New York. W. Durell, 1971. Reprint, Boston, Bedford Books 1995.

European Architecture Series, Eiffel Tower, Paris. https://www.visual-arts-cork.com/architecgure/eiffel-towrhtm,. Accessed 11/30/19.

Jerusalem. History.com, https://www.history.com/topics/ancient-middle-east/history-of-jerusalem, accessed 6/17/20.

Jerusalem-End of the Gentile Age. God 1ˢᵗ Bible Fellowship, https://www.God1st.org/Jerusalem-End-of-the-Gentile-Age, accessed 6/15/20.

Munroe, Myles, and Benny Hinn. *Dr. Myles Munroe discusses Kingdom Paradigm with Benny Hinn (Seg 1 of 2).* YouTube, 1 Kingdom for All, October 3, 2014, https://m.youtube.com/watch22?v=lun7SRj22ZE.

Munroe, Myles, and Benny Hinn. *Dr. Myles Munroe discusses Kingdom paradigm with Benny Hinn (segment 2 of 2).* YouTube, 1 Kingdom for All, October 15, 2014, https://m.youtube.com/watch?y=LNsArJ8Qv8g.

Munroe, Myles. *Kingdom Principles, Preparing for Kingdom Experience and Expansion.* Shippensburg PA: Destiny Image Publishers, Inc., 2006.

Pushback. Wikipedia, https://www.En.m.wikipedia.org/wiki/Pushback, Accessed 4/27/20.

The Perfect Storm, directed by Wolfgang Petersen, 2000, based on the nonfiction book by Sebastian Junger. See also https://en.m.wikipedia.org/wiki/The_Perfect_Storm_(film), accessed 1/15/19.